# Accountability

# Accountability
## Getting a Grip on Results

Second Edition

**Bruce Klatt,
Shaun Murphy and David Irvine**

Co-published in 1998 by RedStone Publishing
1801 – 8 Street S.W., Calgary, Alberta, Canada T2T 2Z2
Telephone: (403) 228·0880  Fax: (403) 245·8725

and

Stoddart Publishing Co. Limited
34 Lesmill Road, Toronto, Canada M3B 2T6
Telephone: (416) 445·3333  Fax: (416) 445·5967

First edition published in 1997 by RedStone.

**CANADIAN CATALOGUING IN PUBLICATION DATA**

Klatt, Bruce
Accountability

2nd edition
ISBN 0-7737-6012-1

1. Management. 2. Responsibility. I. Murphy, Shaun David, 1947– II. Irvine, David, 1956– III. Title.

HD58.7.K52 1998     658.4     C98-931461-8

Design and Production: Jeremy Drought / Last Impression Publishing Service
Cover adapted from an original design by Gherkin Studios
Authors' Photos: Dwayne Brown Studio
Editor: Janet Alford


Printed and bound in Canada

*We dedicate this book to our children:*

*Bryan, Jeff, Ryan, Shane, Mellissa, Hayley and Chandra.*
*Together we are on a path of learning about accountability.*

# Table of Contents

*"Finally, personal mastery teaches us to choose. Choosing is a courageous act: picking the results and actions which you will make into your destiny."*

— Peter Senge
*The 5th Discipline Fieldbook*

# Why Accountability?

■ *The principles of accountability, as practiced through the application of Accountability Agreements, bring structure, focus and clarity to human endeavours in organizations.*

■ *Accountability closes the gap between intention and action.*

■ *In modern life, the art of fan dancing is in better shape than the ability to demand accountability. Hardly anyone tells anyone else to shape the hell up, then takes the trouble to make sure they do.* — **Owen Edwards**

■ *Accountability makes business respectable; it is the foundation for an ethical business culture.*

■ *Accountable people are aware of, and willing to live with, the positive and negative consequences of their actions. If they want different consequences, they take different actions.*

■ *Accountability and empowerment are inseparable.*

■ *Accountability is a promise and an obligation, both to yourself and to the people around you, to deliver specific, defined results.*

## Accountability is about shared achievement

*People need tools to manage interdependence effectively.*

*Nothing is so practical as a good theory.*

**Kurt Lewin**

THE moment a group of people organize to achieve a desired result, the members of that group become interdependent. Inevitably, interdependence requires some kind of structure: roles, goals, agreements, schedules, and the like. The structure may be implied, or it may be spelled out in detail. Regardless of the size or purpose of the organization—be it a small community association, an entrepreneurial service business, or a mammoth multinational corporation—success will always depend on people holding themselves, and each other, accountable. As members of organizations, we are accountable: to keep our commitments to one other, to fulfill our roles in the organization, and most importantly, to achieve agreed-upon results.

In some organizations, interdependence is managed easily, informally, and with little structure. People are readily available to talk with each other daily, if not hourly. As a result, expectations can be continuously clarified and relationships strengthened. Misunderstandings are uncovered and resolved quickly, before time and resources are wasted, and before people become frustrated with each other's action or lack thereof. Course corrections happen in real time, as needed.

In most organizations, however, some structure is essential to effective interdependence. The organization may be large and the relationships complex, or the organization may be small and the relationships intense. Either way, people often lack the time, tools, skills, or inclination to continuously clarify expectations and resolve misunderstandings. The principles of accountability, as practiced through the application of Accountability Agreements, bring structure, focus, and clarity to human endeavours in organizations. This is our purpose.

The theory and tools in this book build accountability. Accountability, in turn, builds relationships that get results.

## How organizations undermine results

A S participants in and managers of organizations, we often lack the tools to build accountability. The consequences are easy to spot. Most readers will recognize their own versions of these real life experiences:

■ An organization becomes comfortably stuck in a culture of non-performance. It becomes an "open secret" that goal-setting is nothing more than a meaningless paper exercise or game. People learn all the acceptable organizational excuses for explaining why they didn't achieve their goals. Rationalization and excuses are offered and accepted in lieu of results.

■ Mistakes are visibly punished and not soon forgotten. Risk-taking is labelled a kamikaze sport, for fools only. Errors are avoided at all costs or at least covered up quickly. Innovation is absent and little learning takes place. Cautious activity replaces results.

■ Motivational rewards for exceptional performance barely exceed rewards for the ordinary. To ensure average performers don't feel short-changed, to save evaluation time, to keep costs down, rewards fail to recognize results.

■ Despite extensive effort from participants, a joint employee-management task force proposal is shelved without explanation. The rumor-mill is active but senior management remains tight-lipped and uncommunicative. Excessive control buries results.

■ Managers stifle what they know to be true in order to live by a culture of excessive politeness. In the interests of a superficial harmony, marginal performance is overlooked and thereby subtly reinforced. Avoiding embarrassment and "getting along" replace results.

■ A senior manager's abusive behaviour is covered up by his transfer to another department. Nothing more is said regarding the matter. Employees begin to doubt management's depth of commitment to respect and fair treatment. Denial undermines results.

The concept and experience of accountability need rejuvenation. We hear that corporations need to be more accountable, teachers need to be more accountable, employees need to be more accountable. You'd almost think we understand each other when we use this term. Yet unless we clarify accountable to whom, for what specific results, and with what consequences, accountability remains an illusion. The principles of accountability stay just out of reach; its potential hovers just beyond our grasp.

## What we offer, and why a second edition

THIS book explains the process for using Accountability Agreements to instill, build, and support accountability in organizations. We have used Accountability Agreements with all types of organizations, and we have seen the results time and time again. Our intention is to provide a stimulating place to begin a conversation about accountability.

We write to leaders. We know that leaders can be found anywhere in an organization, at every pay grade and in any department. Leaders are defined by action, not size of office. Leaders *challenge* the process, *inspire* shared vision, *enable* others to act, *model* the way, and *encourage* the heart (in the words of Kouzes and Posner).

As with any leadership tool, the effective use of Accountability Agreements requires an understanding of the principles involved. This book will help leaders to:

- Understand the power, the benefits, and the risks of accountability.
- Consider the leadership challenge inherent in building accountability.
- Develop and write your own Accountability Agreement.
- Implement Accountability Agreements in your organization.

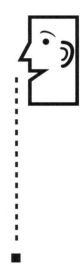

We challenge you to hear the word *accountability* as if you have never really heard it before. We challenge you to suspend your preconceived notions. In the deluge of management fads, we all get buried in buzzwords which carry no meaning. We wish to rescue accountability from this quagmire.

The first edition of this book expressed our understanding of accountability at a point in time. We offer this second edition to share more of what we have learned from our clients and readers. Accountability is a rich and intricate concept, ripe with subtle nuances, unanticipated implications, and opportunities for deeper learning. As a result of publishing our ideas, we have seen them applied in new and diverse ways. Thus this edition also includes a considerably expanded range of real life examples.

*Leadership is the multiplication of hope.*
**Peter Barsukov,
Lukoil, Moscow**

In the ideal world we envision, accountability has become a valued, well-understood, widely-practiced, and enduring characteristic of business and corporate culture. To that end, we offer our contribution.

# The Key Principles of Accountability

A T the foundation of any business transaction is the premise of a *fair deal*. Since the dawn of human history, the fair deal has made trade possible. This is as true in an international agreement involving billions of dollars as it is in the purchase of bread from the corner store. The desire and demand for *quid pro quo*, one thing in fair exchange for another, underscores all business dealings—including the transaction we call employment.

In complex organizational relationships, it is all too easy to lose sight of the terms of this trade. On the surface, the employer/employee relationship is a fair deal wherein the employer's money is traded for the employee's time and talent. The deeper reality, however, is that the employer is actually trading *resources* for a set of desirable *results*, which the employee is expected to deliver. Yet the employee is often managed as though what matters is time and talent, rather than results. The fair deal or trade between today's knowledge worker and his or her employer is much more subtle, and complex to manage, than the fair deal between shopper and shopkeeper.

Furthermore, the complexity in this fair deal is increasing. As many observers have noted, our knowledge-based society requires creativity, commitment to results, judgment, and discretion from its workforce. Production workers, who are expected to simply stay in their roles and do what they're told, are increasingly rare. The terms of the employment transaction become fuzzier as the need for judgment and discretion on-the-job becomes greater. What product or result, exactly, is a "knowledge worker" expected to deliver?

*Any job is simply a business bargain −a trade.*

Accountability Agreements equip leaders and managers to focus the complexity within their organizations. This tool transforms an often-unspoken and easily misunderstood business bargain into explicit expectations, promises, outcomes, and consequences. A well-negotiated agreement will explain to people who work together, either as employer and employee or as peers, what fair deal is being acted out in terms of results expected and produced, and rewards expected and received. (We use the term *employee* to include all those in the employ of an organization, be they senior executives, middle managers, technical professionals, or part-time students.)

An Accountability Agreement becomes a specific personal commitment between an individual and his or her manager, peers, team members, and customers. Six key principles form the foundation for understanding accountability. Each principle is essential, and will be discussed in some detail. Together, they form a practical theory of accountability.

*Remember, all commerce, both social and economic, is based on the principle of exchange —giving something and getting something else.*

**S.M. Campbell**

- Accountability is a statement of personal promise.
- Accountability for results means activities aren't enough.
- Accountability for results requires room for personal judgment and decision-making.
- Accountability is neither shared nor conditional.
- Accountability for the organization as a whole belongs to everyone.
- Accountability is meaningless without consequences.

# The First Key Principle:
## Accountability is a statement of personal promise.

BEING accountable within an organization means you agree to be operationally defined as the sole agent for an outcome, regardless of the (very often inadequate) level of authority or control which you have available. Accountability is a *promise* and an *obligation*, both to yourself and to the people around you, to deliver specific, defined results. Accountability demands that each member of the organization "step up to the plate." Accountability, as we define it, does not apply to departments, work groups, or entire organizations. Accountability applies to *individuals*. This is first and foremost a personal commitment, to the organization and to those the organization serves.

To operate from a position of accountability is to recognize that each person stands in the centre of a circle of influence, and to be willing to push that circle of influence outwards in pursuit of results. It is more than just trying, doing your best, or behaving in certain ways. Accountability is an empowering mindset for people in organizations. Needless to say, it is naïve to empower people who are not focused on results, or who don't know what results they are expected to achieve. So accountability, as you will see, also requires that each member of the organization knows, clearly and specifically, what results he or she is promising to achieve.

*The principle of accountability takes precedence over all others.*

■

*If I am not for myself, who am I for? But if I am only for myself, who am I?*
**Jewish proverb**

■

*Accountability, simply defined, is the awareness and acceptance of the positive and negative consequences of our behavior.*

■

## The Second Key Principle:
## Accountability for results means activities aren't enough.

I F it's your area, function, or project, you are accountable. The organization is depending on a set of results and you have made a personal promise to deliver. That's your fair deal. Everyone in an organization, from the Chief Executive Officer to the janitor, has some piece of the business and a corresponding set of results which are theirs to achieve. Busyness is not enough. Accountability for results is more than simply completing a list of activities.

Distinguishing *results* from *activities* requires a shift in thinking, built on awareness of *why* we do *what* we do. Traditional job descriptions are worded in terms of activities. Rarely do they mention results. An accountant's job description, for example, includes *activities* such as "conducting efficient audits" or "preparing bank reconciliations." An accountant's Accountability Agreement, on the other hand, speaks about a broader, more powerful *result* such as "the financial integrity of the organization." Consider another example. The typical supervisor's job description includes *activities* such as "training," "performance evaluations," and "timely communication." In contrast, any supervisor's Accountability Agreement includes a result such as "the success of all direct reports."

Inasmuch as accountability averts organizational "firefighting," real firefighters provide a great example. Think about *activities* versus *results* for firefighters. If your house is on fire, you need results. *Put out the fire and protect the people, fast!* Imagine your reaction if the firefighter were to complete the prescribed list of activities—blast the siren, drive fast, hook up the water, run up the ladder, guide the hose—and then drive away, fire blazing. Of course, that's not what happens. The

*Accountability Agreements are a leadership tool for clarifying, negotiating, and communicating each person's business within the business.*

firefighter doesn't just perform a list of activities. The firefighter does whatever is necessary to achieve results. There's no leaving until everyone is safe and the fire is permanently out. That's accountability.

---

### Accountability and Responsibility

One caveat about the term *accountability* is worth noting. No sooner will you begin talking about it than someone will ask how this is different from *responsibility*. Some authors (for example Martin, 1995) make the distinction that only managers are accountable, whereas individual contributors are responsible. We feel it's a mistake to create two such classes of employees in an organization, with the implication that accountability is the sole domain of management.

We think of the terms *accountability* and *responsibility* as essentially synonymous. However, we avoid using the word responsibility in this context. It has lost most of its impact through years of being over-used and under-applied. Too often, someone uses the word *responsibility* and people stop listening. The concept of accountability, although similar in its denotation, has a much more powerful connotation. It attracts attention. People can listen with fresh ears.

---

## The Third Key Principle:
## Accountability for results requires room for personal judgment and decision-making.

IF you're not allowed to use any judgment or discretion on the job, if you're told to follow the rules no matter what, if no decision is up to you, then your boss can only hold you accountable for activities. You can be held accountable for doing what you're told, but you can't be held accountable for the outcome. Accountability Agreements are of minimal value in this situation. Conversely, these agreements are invaluable where people have room to exercise personal judgment and make

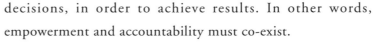

decisions, in order to achieve results. In other words, empowerment and accountability must co-exist.

Two types of errors are relevant to this discussion (from a classification developed by Charles Handy). Type-1 error is simply "getting it wrong." In a black-and-white, rule-following work environment, a type-1 error is nothing more than a failure to follow standard procedure. If it's standard procedure in your company to get the purchasing department's approval before you buy a new computer, and you don't, then you've made a type-1 error. If it's standard procedure to fill a customer order within 48 hours, and you do, then you've avoided a type-1 error. (The computer's capacity to meet your needs, or the customer's satisfaction with 48-hour turnaround, is not the issue. Following the rules is.) If you're only concerned with type-1 error, Accountability Agreements may not be of much value, because type-1 error is relatively easy to avoid. The bureaucrat who does everything by the book avoids type-1 error. Personal judgment and decision-making are neither required nor particularly welcome.

*If it's your area, you're accountable.*

**Paula Martin**

Type-2 error is more complex. A type-2 error is "not getting it right," or at least not getting it right enough. It's about the failure to achieve *results*. If you are buying a computer to solve a specific problem in your office, and the computer you choose is inappropriate to the task, then you've made a type-2 error (whether or not you consulted with the purchasing department). If an important customer expresses a one-time need for 12-hour delivery and you fail to respond, you may have followed the rules but you've still made a type-2 error. Avoiding type-2 error requires discretion, judgment, and innovation.

*People will increasingly demand to take part in choices that affect their lives.*

**C.A. Rogers**

Judgment and innovation (like creativity, risk-taking, and decision-making) can never be fully described in a job description or a procedures manual. These behaviors and attitudes are the hallmarks of knowledge-work. In organizations committed to avoiding type-2 error, employees are expected to do much more than just what they're told. Employees are expected to be resourceful in the achievement of *results*. In this environment, people are held accountable for the things they could have done, but didn't.

Picture a dog on a leash, or a horse on a lead. Leashes and leads severely limit freedom. Now picture the dog running free inside a fenced yard, or the horse roaming an enclosed pasture. Room for personal judgment and decision-making means being on the loose inside the pasture. There are limits (the agreed-upon extent of your accountabilities) and there is room to move.

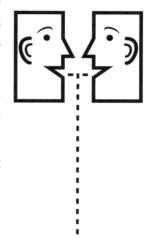

*Accountability doesn't mean you have full control, and not having full control doesn't lessen your accountability.*

## The Fourth Key Principle:
## Accountability is neither shared nor conditional.

THE Accountability Agreement is an individual, unique, personal strategy. Accountability is not *committee-ized*. We recommend that no two people hold the same accountability. Separating each person's accountabilities can be challenging, but remarkable clarity results from the struggle to eliminate overlap. Of course, the challenge is greatest where employees are highly interdependent. This may feel a bit like separating Siamese twins. In the end, however, you will have built more than just role clarity. Interdependencies, support requirements, and individual accountability for results will have been agreed upon, committed to, and communicated throughout the organization.

Accountability is unconditional on several levels; it exists regardless of limited control, or others' mistakes, or lack of role clarity. Limited control is a fact of everyone's life. Being accountable for "minimal downtime" in a production facility doesn't mean you can stop lightning from striking. The inability to control lightning, however, doesn't lessen your accountability. You can, and must, consider the possibility of lightning, assess the risk, buy lightning rods and fire insurance, re-think that computer back-up system, and train staff in emergency procedures. People behave differently if they accept accountability for all eventualities within their area; they will be alert to possible surprises because they are accountable for outcomes, not just activities.

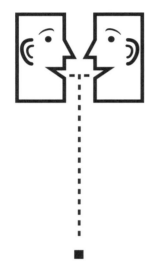

A portion of your accountability can be assigned (to a direct report, a peer, or perhaps a contractor) but, paradoxically, accountability cannot be disowned. You retain accountability for that which you have assigned. Thus a leader is accountable for the success of followers, and for the mistakes made by those followers (regardless of whether they are direct reports, contractors, or report lower in the hierarchy). Although we encourage pushing accountability down to the lowest possible levels in an organization, unlike decision-making, delegating accountability also means retaining it. You may hold a subordinate accountable for a portion of your results, but you are also fully accountable for those results. Regardless of how

*Delegating a portion of your accountability does not relieve you of this accountability.*

much you delegate, if it's your department, project, or job, then you are accountable, end of story.

Suppose, for example, that you select a manager to lead a significant project in your department. If that manager makes poor decisions, you are accountable for the choice of this person as project leader. You may experience the consequences of a failed project in terms of lost revenue to your department or company, and in terms of lost credibility as a leader who can identify and support talented people. This becomes more true as you become more senior in an organization. The choice of key executives influences the overall success of the entire organization. It's an important area of accountability.

Finally, although accountability needs to be negotiated in organizations, there are no excuses for "not knowing" what results you are expected to achieve. If your boss won't work with you to define your accountability, then it's up to you to keep testing the boundaries until you're told to stop. As you experiment, your area of accountability becomes, if not clear, at least better defined and understood.

*Take your life*
*in your hands*
*and what happens?*
*A terrible thing:*
*no one to blame.*
**Erica Jong**

## The Fifth Key Principle:
## Accountability for the organization as a whole belongs to everyone.

THE acid test of commitment in an organization (as described by Perry, Stot & Smallwood, 1993) is passed when a manager gives up people or resources to another department, or to a project outside his area, because this is best for the organization as a whole. Every employee is accountable for thinking about and acting on what is best for the organization, even if doing so means putting aside one's individual, functional, or departmental accountability. Individual accountability does not mean individual fiefdoms.

## Who's Accountable?

One of our partners, Dave Irvine, does a lot of speaking to large groups internationally, usually as part of a major conference held in a hotel. On his arrival, he often used to find that the requested room set-up and equipment wasn't ready. This is no small problem. When you're about to speak to five hundred people, you need to concentrate on the job at hand, not the microphone.

As he reviewed procedures, Dave realized why things were going wrong. There were always several people involved in coordinating these events, none of whom had clear accountability for logistics. Sometimes Dave made his arrangements with the hotel staff directly. Sometimes his office manager would handle the logistical details. Occasionally a third-party meeting planner was involved. Needless to say, there was plenty of opportunity for any one of a number of people to drop the ball.

Dave is accountable for the success of his presentations, so it was up to him to do something besides blame others. He explained his logistical requirements to his office manager, and made her accountable for the desired result: "well-organized events." She started making all arrangements personally, and initiated pre-event confirmation meetings to ensure all the details were in hand every time. Dave's speaking engagement logistics are now working well. The key, it turned out, was clear accountability.

Another of our partners, Shaun Murphy, does a great deal of management consulting in other countries, particularly in Russia. Shaun relies on the assistance of language interpreters as he conducts his work in a cross-cultural, cross-language setting.

Shaun knows that he is accountable for accurate, appropriate communication with his international clients and their employees. Although the language interpreter is accountable for the correct and timely translation of Shaun's and others' words, Shaun holds the overall accountability for effective communication. Therefore, Shaun must find interpreters who can work comfortably in his business setting. He must practice with his interpreter in advance, making statements and asking the interpreter to repeat back what he or she has heard. He must develop a working rapport with his interpreter. He must ask for feedback regarding cultural differences and sensitivities. In order to do his work, Shaun depends on the support of an interpreter, but it is Shaun who is accountable for effective communication.

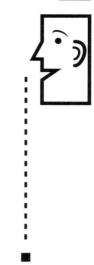

This is the one place where shared accountability is acceptable, indeed essential. The most successful organizations expect and allow every person to be of practical assistance in realizing the organization's goals.

For example, if sales decrease the manufacturing department may need to slow down production, even though it will fail to achieve production targets as a result. Otherwise, the cost of carrying finished products in inventory becomes a considerable burden on the company's cash flow. Failing to make such a production decision could damage the entire organization, perhaps fatally. The head of the manufacturing department has an *accountability for the organization as a whole.*

We have consulted in organizations where the principle of accountability to the whole was not respected. In one case, two senior executives were acting out a nasty, damaging turf war. Neither was willing to surrender, not to the organization's overall good, and certainly not to each other. The dispute lasted over a year, with extremely negative effects on the departments involved. Ultimately, the CEO asked both executives to clarify their accountabilities to him, to each other, and to the senior management group. They were reluctant to do so, and when they were finished it was obvious that these executives accepted no accountability to the organization as a whole. In this case there was no easy solution; the CEO fired the more intransigent of the two.

Reconsider our earlier analogy of the dog and fenced yard (not that we wish to over-extend the dog metaphor). The dog is not living behind a ten-foot concrete wall. He can see and hear through the fence, is aware of what's going on beyond his defined space, and will get over or under the fence if needed. Accountability is neither an excuse to create a protectionist turf mentality, nor an opportunity to ignore the bigger picture.

*Most of us act like we are just renting our jobs, so we don't give the job the same care and attention that we give to something we own.*

*How many people pay the same attention to maintaining a rental car as they pay to maintaining their own?*

*How many people wash a rental car before returning it to the rental agency?*

**Jim Kouzes**

## The Sixth Key Principle:
## Accountability is meaningless without consequences.

CONSEQUENCES are that which you earn, receive, or are denied, based on the results realized in your area of accountability. Sometimes consequences are *natural* or inevitable, other times they are *arbitrary*. Neither of these is our focus. In Accountability Agreements, consequences need to be negotiated. Negotiated consequences can be *positive* or *negative*. The following examples will help clarify what we mean:

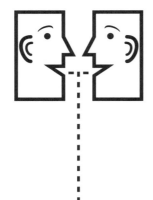

■ Sales in your department increase by 15%. As a *negotiated positive consequence*, you receive a significant year-end bonus.

■ You haven't come anywhere near your promise to reduce costs by 10%. As a *negotiated negative consequence*, you temporarily lose some of your freedom to manage; senior management requires you to follow a strict regimen of cost control.

■ The project you've been leading for the past year is completed on time and under budget. Everyone is happy with the results. As a *negotiated positive consequence*, your boss offers you a choice of two highly-sought assignments. You now have an enviable and difficult choice to make.

*Consequences are the heart and soul of accountability.*

■ An employee survey uncovers a sharp downturn in morale, particularly in the department you manage. As a *negotiated negative consequence*, you are not eligible for promotion or transfer within the next year. This is not based on an arbitrary whim. You and your boss have agreed that you need to develop and demonstrate leadership ability where you are, before you move on to manage another part of the organization.

Negotiated consequences that are personally significant to the employee in question are an essential element of Accountability Agreements. They are fundamental to the *fair deal*. We cannot emphasize this enough. Without the incentive of negotiated consequences, accountability is meaningless. No matter how often the word is mentioned in speeches, memos, or executive presentations, accountability divorced from consequences is quite simply bogus.

Negotiated consequences are explicit bargains made with yourself, your boss, or your work group. They are tailored to the individual and the organization. In many organizations, this is a senior management issue. Not just anyone can reward achievements, deny salary increases, or offer promotions. Financial rewards, of course, aren't the only personally significant consequence which the organization can offer. What are those things, aside from compensation, that influence job satisfaction? The answer is as individual as the people in organizations.

*Accountability is not about assigning blame.*

Perhaps, if you achieve the desired results in your area of accountability, the organization agrees to sponsor your participation at a number of professional development programs. If you're self-employed, you might promise yourself a Caribbean cruise if you achieve a result such as reaching a given income level or publishing a book. While one employee might value football tickets in return for results achieved, another might find more reward in receiving a few additional vacation days, or in public recognition for his or her

*Negotiated consequences are agreed upon in advance and represent a fair trade for results achieved.*

accomplishments. (Further examples of consequences can be found under step six of "Write an Accountability Agreement" later in this volume.)

Not all negotiated consequences will require significant resources, but some will. Certainly, tailoring consequences to individual taste will require a creative, flexible approach to rewards and recognition programs. This can be difficult in traditional, bureaucratic organizations, where compensation and incentive programs are tightly constrained and even the smallest change requires several layers of management approval. Accountability Agreements may be of less value in such a setting. Yet even in these organizations, accountability can have an impact—provided that employees are allowed some room for decision-making, and that some modest opportunity for negotiated consequences can be created.

*Praise is not plutonium ... spread it around.*

## What We Don't Mean By Consequences

Some of our clients react negatively to the word *consequences*. We encourage you to resist the temptation to confuse consequences with punishment. These terms are not synonymous. Negotiated consequences in Accountability Agreements may be positive or negative, but either way they need to be *fair*. They are not punishing, under-handed, or capricious. Finding out what went wrong in a situation is useful for preventing the recurrence of problems, but accountability is not about assigning after-the-fact blame. Rather, it's about providing before-the-fact incentive for success, and room for decision-making, risk-taking and growth. Given this people will, on occasion, fall short of optimum results. On other occasions, they will succeed at levels far beyond what anyone thought possible.

## What We Don't Mean By Consequences – Continued

*Arbitrary consequences* result from a decision made by someone in authority, without consultation or explanation. These are inconsistent with the principles of accountability. It's an arbitrary consequence when you are unexpectedly taken off a project because you didn't generate a particular short-term result, even though you didn't push for that result because you believed it wasn't important. It's also an arbitrary consequence when your boss increases your annual bonus but you're not clear why. Arbitrary consequences always exist in organizations, but they are minimized when Accountability Agreements are well-defined.

*Natural consequences*, the inevitable results of your decisions and actions, will flow regardless of whether, or how well, you have defined your accountabilities. These, therefore, are also generally not the focus of Accountability Agreements. If you work on a team and are unable to deliver on an important promise, for example, you may naturally suffer a loss of standing. If you build effective relationships with key decision makers, you are naturally more likely to find an audience for your ideas or recommendations. These consequences are important to people in organizations, but they are not subject to negotiation.

Many people are inclined to include natural consequences in their Accountability Agreements. This is all right, as long as natural consequences don't completely replace negotiated consequences. *The element of negotiation is critical.* Also, notice that the closer you are to an ownership position in the organization, the more important natural consequences become. The natural consequence of serving or not serving an important customer will be felt in the pocketbook of the entrepreneur or owner much more quickly that it will be felt in the pocketbook of most employees. Even entrepreneurs or owners, however, need to negotiate consequences for (and often with) themselves.

# 3 The Benefits, the Risks, and the Shadow Side

## The Benefits

OVER the past several years we have helped many organizations to use Accountability Agreements as a way of clarifying the *quid pro quo* of a fair business deal between employees and their organizations. We have come to appreciate the power of these agreements, the commitment and open communication they generate, and the benefits to both employees and their organizations. The range of benefits is profound, and includes:

- Improving role clarity, and facilitating the negotiation of expectations, interdependencies, gaps, and overlaps in work.
- Creating room for decision-making and personal growth.
- Providing a context for goal-setting.
- Building a rationale for decisions about organizational structure and design.
- Enabling people to let go of whatever is not their accountability.
- Enhancing commitment to outcomes.

*Accountability Agreements provide freedom, focus, and reassurance.*

Accountability Agreements will help you focus your efforts, and the efforts of your employees and team members. They do this by clarifying purpose, roles, results sought, and relationships within an organization. Because accountability flows up, down and sideways, if others also use this tool these agreements will improve communication and coordination throughout your organization.

As we have suggested, job descriptions are insufficient in an environment where knowledge-workers are expected to use judgment and discretion on the job. Knowledge-workers conceptualize problems and opportunities, devise solutions, and plan implementation. Their contribution (as noted by Robert Reich) depends on quality, originality, cleverness, and leadership. Specifying activities and assigning duties, when you want employees to show leadership, is more than a little contradictory. The real value that knowledge-workers add in organizations comes from what might be called *extra-role* behaviours. These behaviours require initiative, risk-taking, creativity, and teamwork. They are spontaneous expressions which flow from the employee's commitment: to the organization, to the profession, and to the personal satisfaction in work well done. Rarely can such extra-role behaviors be specified in advance.

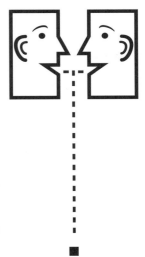

By defining clear roles and goals, as opposed to simple descriptions of activities, Accountability Agreements focus energy. They define the parameters within which judgment and discretion are encouraged. They specify the obligation, opportunity, and challenge to achieving results. The process builds a more informed, confident, and empowered work force. Accountability Agreements also clarify interdependencies, and can be used to negotiate differences where boundaries between employees are unclear or in dispute.

This tool reassures people that they can trust others to follow through on agreements, meet deadlines, and add value for customers. Organizational members become more confident that promises, once made, will be taken seriously and kept.

*The Accountability Agreement is a powerful tool for discovering a deeper meaning in what you do.*

## Comparing Accountability Agreements, Management By Objectives (MBO), and Traditional Job Descriptions

| Accountability Agreement | MBO | Job Description |
|---|---|---|
| Legitimizes and emphasizes discussion of positive and negative consequences. Recognizes the quid pro quo inherent in the business bargain that we have traditionally called "a job." | If any attention is paid to consequences, it is likely to be nothing more than a component of the standard compensation/reward package offered in the organization. | Consequences are exclusively within the domain of the employer. They are not negotiable. The standard compensation package is primarily based on years of service and job level. |
| A strategic orientation towards the individual's "business within the business." | Strategic direction may be assumed but is de-emphasized. Concentrates on measuring key elements of success within current context. | Considers neither goals nor strategic focus. |
| Insistence that the employer/employee relationship is adult to adult. | Allows "role-playing" of an adult-to-adult relationship but within the traditional context which remains heavily parent/child oriented. | Traditional parent/child orientation. (The golden rule: he who has the gold makes the rules.) |
| Tailored to the individual's strengths. | May consider some of the individual's strengths. | Focused on the traditional definition of a job. Ignores the uniqueness of the individual job incumbent. |
| Takes a broad, results-oriented and entrepreneurial perspective. | A narrow yet results-oriented focus. | Looks only at the package of tasks or activities called "a job." Ignores outcomes for customers. |
| Considers the big picture (all accountabilities) as well as specific goals within a given time period. | Focuses only on specific goals within a given time period. | Focuses only on activities, competencies, past experience, and formal education. No significance attached to goals or results. |
| Formal recognition that obligations and accountabilities flow in many directions. "Support agreements" spell out accountabilities flowing to the individual. | Ignores accountabilities of others (immediate supervisor, peers, direct reports) to the job holder. | Doesn't consider accountabilities at any level or in any direction. |

---

**With Practice, Being Accountable Becomes a Way of Life**

As Dave was working on this book, his three year old daughter, Hayley, came into the office to ask if Daddy would play with her. "In five minutes," Dave responded. "I've just got one more thought to finish up here." Dave handed Hayley his watch, saying, "I need you to wait until the last number is an eight."

Hayley sat quietly on the floor, watching intently as the numbers changed on Daddy's watch. Finally, the number eight arrived. She jumped up in excitement and yelled, "It's time to play, Daddy!" Dave wasn't finished with his thought yet, but he was abruptly reminded of his accountability. He had made an agreement, and now it was time to follow through.

---

## The Risks

FOR some, accountability is a loaded concept. It implies being judged. Accountability Agreements have grip. They accept no excuses. An accountable person is trusted, and is therefore given the resources and freedom necessary to make decisions on behalf of the organization. These agreements:

- Put traction between intention and action. Accountability Agreements are public documents within (and often outside) the organization. Everyone knows what others are accountable for.
- Are exclusive to one person. Accountabilities are not committee-ized or syndicated.
- Are unconditional. Accountabilities exist twenty-four hours a day, regardless of circumstances.
- Are predicated on trust and support.

The truth is this may scare some people. Depending on an individual's maturity, independence, and openness to learning, an employee may see two risks in Accountability Agreements:

■ The Accountability Agreement carries the burden of a promise made. It is explicit about the results each person is expected to achieve, regardless of circumstances.

■ By demanding more in terms of judgment, discretion and initiative, Accountability Agreements provide more room for decision-making, and therefore more room for error.

Accountability Agreements require a public commitment, and that commitment comes with consequences. If you are not committed to results, you will eventually experience loss, because with Accountability Agreements traditional organizational excuses cease to be an option.

Building genuine accountability will involve a good deal of cultural change for many organizations. Employees and managers will be required to change their expectations of, and relationship to, one other. Thus, Accountability Agreements will only appeal to those who have considerable goodwill toward their organizations, and who have the trust and mutual respect needed to openly challenge each other to achieve business results, and to develop personally and professionally.

*With Accountability Agreements, goals become personal promises. It's a matter of integrity.*

Some managers will see this tool as involving too much obligation, being too risky. After all, if you ask those reporting to you to be accountable, and if you work with them to clearly specify this accountability and its consequences, then they will expect you, the manager, to be accountable as well. This upward flow of accountability is often the hidden benefit for direct reports, but it also deliberately creates some friction in the hierarchy.

## The Games Organizations Play

Organizations often have subtle unwritten codes regarding excuses. This becomes clear when we consider people's attitudes toward the organization's annual plan. In many organizations, people (including those who wrote the plan) do not really expect to see the plan's objectives fully accomplished. There is a certain amount of slack built in, in a before-the-fact effort to compensate for a presumed lack of commitment.

The executive notion, often unstated, is "If we create so-called stretch targets, we'll know they are unrealistic and be less disappointed when they're not achieved, as opposed to setting targets that are realistic and attainable and then not achieving those. In addition, employees will have to work harder to minimize their disappointment."

Workers also play this game. "If management set ten units of production as the target, it means that they are really expecting about eight, and will likely not be surprised if they get seven. If we actually deliver ten they will feel the target was too low!"

This leads us to describe the organization's annual plan as the yearly *corporate lie*, since no one in the organization believes the plan will really unfold as written. Nonetheless, it would be disloyal to actually say so. This generates an atmosphere of game-playing and insincerity. People are unsure what others have committed to, or are capable of delivering, creating the opportunity for sophisticated and negative organizational politics. Out of necessity, people operate with tacit assumptions and insider confidences such as, "if you say that it was a human resources problem, they'll accept that you couldn't achieve your goal."

Such an organization may find that it is perpetually trying to solve recurring human resources problems! The solution lies in recognizing that no such "human resources problems" exist, and that framing a lack of results this way is a form of collusion aimed at covering up a culture of excuses.

Imagine the overall waste that such a complex game generates! What if people actually negotiated reasonable agreements and targets, so that they could be fully committed to, and accountable for, the outcomes? What if you really believed that people would do what they said they would do? How would that, in turn, affect your own level of risk-taking and performance? What if everyone in an organization were truly committed to the organization's annual plan? What if the annual plan were actually achieved?

## The Shadow Side

Although Accountability Agreements are a powerful vehicle for focusing human energy, like any form of power they are open to misuse. There are at least three ways in which this can happen:

- An unfair bargain can be developed in which the unfairness is made non-discussible.
- Individuals can be tempted to set extremely negative consequences for themselves.
- Incomplete Accountability Agreements can be made to operate exclusively in a top-down fashion, rendering the concept of accountability meaningless.

**An unfair bargain where the unfairness is made non-discussible.**

Employees can sometimes be coerced into voicing commitment to goals which will demand an inordinate amount of time away from other commitments, including family, friends, and community. This is not infrequently accomplished with the help of consultants or team leaders, who may diagnose the failure to achieve goals as a so-called "lack of real commitment." Remedies for this shortcoming can involve manipulative team meetings, where other team members confront the employee with his or her failure to demonstrate the appropriate attitudes required for the team's success. This is sometimes supplemented with a series of non-voluntary coaching sessions in which the person is again grilled about the sincerity of his or her commitment to the goals set by the organization. This pressure to force the employee into an unbalanced and unhealthy life, where the organization's goals subordinate all other aims and obligations, can be highly destructive.

An employee can feel vulnerable. The job is the source of livelihood—perhaps the only financial security for a family. The job is also a primary source of self-esteem, an outlet for creative impulses, and a place to belong. Employees in such circumstances can be easily swayed, frightened, and intimidated. If the basic values of a balanced life and a respect for genuine choice are not protected, a highly destructive aberration of accountability can be institutionalized in an organization. Such organizations put their employees in an untenable situation. Over time a strong sense of resentment, if not reprisal, is likely to appear.

Above all, fairness must govern the process of accountability. Respect for employees as individuals must balance the organization's power to get greater performance from its people. All good faith business dealings, remember, are founded on the principle of a fair deal.

**Individuals who set extremely negative consequences for themselves.**

As an extension of the factors discussed above, it is not unusual for employees to demand more of themselves than their immediate supervisors demand of them. Employees can be tempted to set targets which are unrealistic, or to invite consequences which are not in their own—or the organization's—best interest. We have known executives to suggest that if they did not achieve all of their accountabilities, they should be fired. The employer's role here is to counter this bluster by supporting the setting of fair and reasonable consequences. Further development, training, or coaching is generally appropriate. Firing is generally not.

In organizations where real consequences for performance do not exist, employees often resort to writing vacuous clichés when describing their accountabilities and consequences. To do otherwise is to expose the meaninglessness of the current

*The dangers of psychological technology are often overlooked.*
**C.A. Rogers**

*Above all, fairness must govern the process of accountability.*

performance management system, and the current lack of accountability in the organization. In such a vacuum, it is tempting to adopt a tough-guy position. The employee sets himself up as a committed and courageous organizational hero, since the game involves no real stakes at all. Accountability Agreements written in this heroic and unrealistic fashion can become a trap. With little or no support from their bosses, employees may feel compelled to put their jobs on the line by committing to unrealistic targets. This makes employees vulnerable to the arbitrary exercise of managerial power, which can be justified whenever a boss feels it's time to demonstrate his commitment to accountability.

**Incomplete Accountability Agreements which operate in a top-down fashion.**

If the Accountability Agreement does not include a discussion of the supports required by the employee, the document can represent a sort of arm-twisted promise. Instead of accountability flowing in all directions, accountability becomes nothing more than a top-down bullying process. This will encourage the kind of cat-and-mouse games described earlier, in which employees nod in agreement to targets and plans for which they feel no confidence.

Alternatively, if the consequences section of the Accountability Agreement is omitted, the entire process may become simply a bureaucratic paper chase, which in time collapses under its own weight. We cannot over-stress the fact that there is no genuine accountability without consequences. The difficulty that some employees experience in completing the consequences section of Accountability Agreements is symptomatic of the underlying emptiness of many performance management systems, the inertia and inflexibility of compensation systems, and the traditional thinking and limiting habits of organizational leadership.

# Eight Great Excuses for Why Accountability Won't Work

**4**

IN many organizations, the concept of accountability is received with enthusiasm. Employees and managers are eager to use Accountability Agreements to get a handle on roles and expected results. In some cases, however, the culture of the organization or the mindset of certain individuals just isn't ready for this level of commitment. We've seen this happen at the senior management level, and among the rank and file. Resistance surfaces, often in the form of one or more of the following arguments or excuses.

Our purpose here is to equip "accountability champions" to recognize and challenge the *red herrings of resistance*. In any organization, some forms of resistance are more culturally acceptable than others. Readers might anticipate any or all of the following:

- ■ I can't be accountable without full control or authority.
- ■ We concentrate on processes and competencies, and assume that results will follow.
- ■ I don't have the time (resources, people, energy,…) to take this on. Things change too quickly around here.
- ■ Promises get broken all the time. It's no big deal.
- ■ I don't know what my boss wants, so I can't be accountable.
- ■ My job is too big to be described in terms of accountabilities. All I can do is my best.
- ■ My boss would only use it against me.
- ■ This will have to wait until my boss (the management team, my department, my staff) gets on board.

*Like the fancy footwork of the matador, an excuse is an attempt to sidestep the consequences of having tempted fate. But most business people are smarter than bulls; they don't fall for the fancy footwork.*

**Hendricks & Ludeman**

■

Resistance can be based in personal fear (as we suggested in our previous discussion about the risks of accountability). Resistance can also be a logical, intelligent response to a dysfunctional corporate culture (as we suggested in our previous discussion about the shadow side). We retain a realistic view of corporate culture, even as we debunk the following arguments or excuses. In organizations where a distorted concept of accountability is used as nothing more than a club to beat people, it is simply intelligent behavior to resist accountability—with whatever excuse might work.

# Excuse 1:
# I can't be accountable without full control or authority.

THIS line of thinking dates back to Henri Fayol (1916). Defining authority as the right to give orders, and to enforce them with rewards and penalties, Fayol argued that authority should be matched with corresponding responsibility and vice versa. In his day, Fayol's rational argument was entirely workable. In the age of global markets and discontinuous change, however, where innovation, risk-taking, and initiative are the hallmarks of success, Fayol's formula falls far short of managing, much less motivating, today's knowledge-based workforce. In our world, the *right to give orders* has largely been replaced by the need to facilitate, lead, and exercise influence.

The privilege and essence of accountability in organizations today is rarely accompanied by the elixir of full control, or the opportunity to achieve a specified result simply by command. Is the marketing and sales vice-president accountable if the latest product is a spectacular flop? (Or, for that matter, if it is a spectacular success?) Of course the answer is yes. Can that vice-president control the buying decisions of thousands, or millions, of potential customers? Of course the answer is no. The vice-president doesn't have full control, but that doesn't limit accountability. There are a multitude of opportunities for judgment, discretion, and initiative in this situation: creative identification of customer needs, unique and targeted advertising, and a well-trained sales force are just a few of the most obvious.

What accountability does require is the ability, opportunity and willingness to *influence*. Without the power of influence you can't get much done in organizations today. Without influence, your ability to be accountable is limited. To be able to influence you need freedom to exercise judgment and discretion on the job. The vice-president of marketing and sales, and everyone else in the marketing and sales department, needs the *elbow-room* to decide on the right approach to customers, appropriate pricing, package design, ad campaign timing, and a hundred other factors. If they were waiting for full control in order to achieve results, they'd never bother coming to work in the morning.

## Excuse 2:
## We concentrate on processes and competencies, and assume that results will follow.

THIS is another way of staying stuck, or allowing employees to stay stuck, in activities rather than outcomes. As we've suggested, it's limiting, self-defeating, and disempowering to measure performance based on activities and behaviors. Indeed, much of what knowledge-workers produce that is valuable can't even be defined meaningfully in job descriptions or competency profiles. Conceptualizing opportunities, and devising creative solutions, depends on originality, intelligence, and commitment. You can't capture these in a list of preferred behaviors.

This mindset can also be great cover for fear of delegation, or fear of letting go. Even today, some overly rational and formal reporting structures in traditional organizations equate accountability with control. Those higher up think they have it, and are afraid to give it up. Thus, most decisions tend to be made at the highest possible level, in spite of espoused theory that says decisions are to be pushed down in the organization. From the perspective of those lower in the organization, being able to pass decisions up the line limits personal liability—a comforting thought for employees long schooled in hiding inside large bureaucracies. From the perspective of those at more senior levels, being able to make significant decisions limits reliance on an unruly, or at least unpredictable, workforce. (Knowledge-workers are by their very nature outside of a manager's full control.) The end result is comforting to all concerned, although few would say so publicly. The end result is not, however, conducive to the achievement of results.

# Excuse 3:
# I don't have the time (resources, people, energy,...) to take this on. Things change too quickly around here.

WE agree that accountability is an ambitious undertaking, for it requires a profound shift in attitude. Commitment and courage are essential. Accountability fosters and demands an enterprising and entrepreneurial approach to work. To accept accountability, while recognizing a lack of control, creates tension. That's the nature of meaningful work.

The real challenge, though, is usually at the level of belief and attitude, not at the level of workload. We are willing to bet that the process of negotiating an Accountability Agreement will do more to balance and clarify individual workload than any other management tool. Furthermore, accountability is never a one-way street. Being accountable for results means understanding the support needed to achieve those results, and knowing where that support will come from. This is an integral part of the process. Accountability will make your existing time, resources, people, and energy *more* productive, not *less*. The faster "things change," the more important it is to understand your piece of the business, others' expectations, and your fair deal. Otherwise, the pressure becomes paralyzing. Clarity and empowerment are both stressful *and* invigorating.

## Excuse 4:
## Promises get broken all the time. It's no big deal.

PROMISES do get broken in organizations, for a variety of reasons. Here are a few examples:

- "I didn't understand the urgency. We didn't discuss priorities. "
- "I agreed in order to avoid a confrontation. I have a tough time *saying no*."
- "I need to manage my time better. The urgent often overrides the important."
- "I realize now I procrastinated. I often put off work that makes me anxious."
- "I didn't ask for or get support. I need to be a lot clearer about asking for what I need."
- "Sometimes missing deadlines is simply intelligent behavior. If I met all my deadlines, I would just get loaded down with more work."
- "Around here, it is more important to get along than to get things done."

*Being accountable for results means understanding the support needed to achieve those results, and knowing where that support will come from.*

■ "Whether I work well or poorly makes little difference. My boss has no discretion to reward anyone anyway."

Being accountable means giving up the litany of broken promises. Accountability may demand new personal habits: time management, direct communication, the end of procrastination. It may require individual risk-taking: honest communication, asking for help, saying no. It will only thrive in the context of the fair deal: clear expectations, negotiated consequences, the end of playing games. Human beings experience less stress when they make promises they can keep, and keep the promises they make. The culture of excuses and the culture of accountability are mutually exclusive.

# Excuse 5:
# I don't know what my boss wants, so I can't be accountable.

THIS is the equivalent of that old phrase, "just tell me what to do, boss." Such subservience is out of place at any level in today's organizations. Without question, everyone from front-line staff to the senior management team needs role and goal clarity. That's one of the rewards of the Accountability Agreement process. Pushing for that clarity, however, is the personal responsibility of each member of the organization. If I don't know what fair deal I'm in, that's my problem to solve. It's probably way past time I found out.

The exception to this rule happens when managers play the old control game, "keep them in the dark." In such organizations, information is used to gain power; manipulation is a management strategy; consequences are arbitrary; employees don't and can't "know what bosses want." In this case, accountability is as unattractive as it is unlikely.

Not infrequently, we come across an employee (at any level) who complains about not having enough elbow-room for decision making; but at the same time clearly lacks understanding of and commitment to his or her area of accountability. It's a bad idea to empower employees who are not mature, who don't know (or care) where the organization is going, who don't have a sense of accountability for the whole organization, or who don't have an explicit understanding of their specific area of accountability. "I don't know what they want" is often an early warning sign of *victim thinking*. You can't have it both ways. You can't have your empowerment and your non-accountability too.

## Excuse 6:
## My job is too big to be described in terms of accountabilities. All I can do is my best.

S UCH a statement is symptomatic of a problem with perspective. We worked with a group of dedicated school principals who described their role in terms of "ensuring all students realize their full potential as human beings." Needless to say, parents and the students themselves have a (considerably greater) role in achieving this result. Description of results at this high level is significantly outside the principals' influence. It's too big. It lacks actionable focus.

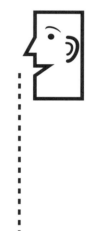

The result of such a problem with perspective is a sense of powerlessness, which fosters an attitude that "all I can do is give it my best effort." Lofty statements, however well-intentioned, have the advantage of sounding ambitious without being connected to any practical circumstance. What's needed is more specific description, significant and challenging but also clear enough to focus energy and guide action. The school principals might better describe their accountability as "ensuring

*To accept accountability, while recognizing a lack of control, creates tension. That's the nature of meaningful work.*

■

students are exposed to an education which motivates and inspires the development of full human potential." This is still a complex and challenging accountability. It is also a result these principals can significantly influence and achieve.

We have said that accountability co-exists with empowerment. Now we want to add that accountability necessitates strategy. Strategy accepts the reality of scarce resources. Individuals and organizations have limits. Grand, ambiguous statements like, "ensuring all students realize their full potential as human beings," or "my role is to meet all the needs of my customers," lack focus. This is not strategy. This is fuzzy and idealistic thinking dressed up to look like strategy. Unless it's exercise you're after, doing your best to chase two rabbits at once is hopeless and frustrating. Both will escape. The rabbit-chaser feels justified in giving up. You can't be accountable without the realistic perspective of a clear strategy. A clear strategy means deciding what is *in*, and what is *out*. You have to decide which rabbit to chase, and which to ignore.

# Excuse 7:
## My boss would only use it against me.

THIS employee fears that an Accountability Agreement will be nothing but a trap. The more I promise, the more they'll expect. Anything I commit to becomes a hammer which can be used against me. This is a fear of old, traditional management at its least attractive (which is still found in some organizations).

Traditional management operates between two extremes. At one extreme, there is little concern for results. What is important is showing up for work, getting along with your boss, following the rules, and creating the appearance of effort. This is bureaucracy at its worst. At the other extreme is the authoritarian boss, for whom any result short of perfection is seen as a punishable failure. Nowhere along this continuum, and certainly not at either extreme, will Accountability Agreements be of much value. On one hand, there is no pressure for results; accountability is irrelevant. On the other hand, there is only perfection or punishment: management by brutality. An employee in either setting would be right to fear the misuse of accountability.

Most organizations now operate in, or are at least moving towards, an atmosphere we describe as *enlightened leadership*. They've left traditional management behind. Enlightened leadership and traditional management are not different by a matter of degree; they operate on completely different foundations. Traditional management views employees from a place of suspicion and control. Enlightened leaders assume that employees want to contribute, and that rewards should be commensurate with results achieved. This stance is completely congruent with the concept of accountability.

*Enlightened leaders play to win. Traditional leaders play not to lose.*

## Excuse 8:
## This will have to wait until my boss (the management team, my department, my staff) gets on board.

FEW people actually "have to wait" for someone else to "get on board." In all but the most rigid organizations, individuals have the potential to innovate, to initiate personal change, and to exercise leadership. In all organizations, there are *positional* leaders, and there are *attitudinal* leaders. The actions of leadership—whether you lead from your position in the hierarchy or by virtue of your attitude—are these (used with gratitude from *The Leadership Challenge* by Jim Kouzes and Barry Posner):

- Challenging the Process
    - search for opportunities
    - experiment and take risks
- Inspiring a Shared Vision
    - envision the future
    - enlist others
- Enabling Others to Act
    - foster collaboration
    - strengthen others
- Modeling the Way
    - set the example
    - plan small wins
- Encouraging the Heart
    - recognize individual contributions
    - celebrate accomplishments

As you see the value in this tool, put it to work for yourself and see what happens. Start by drafting an Accountability Agreement based on your current understanding of your role (more on this under "Write an Accountability Agreement"). Conduct a personal experiment. Share your findings with others. All innovators know that "good ideas have legs."

Accountability is a statement of personal promise. It is a focus on results, not activities. It requires you to push the limits of your influence. These are all shifts which an individual can make—or resist—quite apart from what the rest of the organization is doing. Negotiating consequences with others is essential. As a place to begin, however, what consequences can you negotiate with yourself? Define the support you need, and start to ask for it. Engaging positional leaders in this process is critical, but it's not the only place to begin.

# Take the Leadership Challenge 5

N O tool can serve as a substitute for leadership. No tool will make a real difference in organizations, or in the working lives of individuals, where leadership and commitment are lacking. While our goal is to encourage you to use Accountability Agreements, we recognize that some organizations are better suited to working with these ideas than others. Where there's apathy, any tool, Accountability Agreements included, will fall flat. There are no shortcuts to commitment. People need to be informed, involved, allowed to influence, and given the right to choose for themselves.

In our experience, these are the five essential leadership qualities:

■ Leaders seek commitment, they don't settle for compliance.
■ Leaders focus on results, not activities.
■ Leaders learn, and help others learn, from mistakes.
■ Leaders encourage and challenge, they don't over-control.
■ Leaders reward courage, not caution.

*Many of us complain about the lack of accountability in organizations, yet few of us are prepared to pay the price that is required to hold ourselves and others accountable.*

As we have suggested, leadership arises in many places within an organization. Ultimately, however, Accountability Agreements must be compatible with an organization's culture and supported by key decision-makers if the potential for results is to be realized. Thus, the following section is primarily written to those who hold the privilege and opportunity of designated leadership positions within organizations.

## The First Essential Leadership Quality:
## Leaders seek commitment, they don't settle for compliance.

COMMITMENT underlies success with any tool, Accountability Agreements included. Commitment is about finding the focus and energy to do what it takes to accomplish a goal. This is different from compliance, which connotes a willingness to try, and to follow directions, but lacks the *whatever-it-takes* level of intensity and ownership which is characteristic of commitment.

So, how does one create and support a deep sense of accountability in the workplace? Start by recognizing that commitment is an inside job. Commitment must be felt and accepted. It can't be controlled, manipulated, or coerced. In the words of Hendricks and Ludeman, "you haven't accepted something until you feel a shift deep in yourself ... Accepting is a very comprehensive action. It may take months, not minutes."

*Action without commitment is seldom effective.*

**Karl Weick**

In a culture of ownership and commitment, employees will express their concerns, opinions, and needs directly. If an activity seems meaningless, or does not move the organization toward its purpose, that activity will be challenged long before it uses up valuable time and energy. Accountability Agreements are a great tool in a culture of commitment. They become nothing but a chore in a culture of compliance.

## The Second Essential Leadership Quality:
## Leaders focus on results, not activities.

WE have said that a focus on results, not activities, is a key principle of accountability. This kind of thinking starts at the top. Expect resistance to Accountability Agreements in bureaucratic and steeply hierarchical organizations, where

## Compliance Runs Rampant Inside Large Bureaucracies

Have you ever been promoted, opened a file drawer in your new office, and discovered volumes of reports, analyses and recommendations from a project that has long since died on the vine? Someone must have done a lot of work, hence all the paper. Perhaps circumstances changed, but more likely ownership of the project wasn't strong. Maybe, as the organization began to realize the true cost of this project in terms of time and resources, commitment dwindled. Most likely, a real understanding and deeply felt commitment to the project was never widespread, even though the project may have received a great deal of lip service at one time in its history.

Many organizational improvement initiatives are created with an initial flourish and end up with little more than binders on shelves, reminding people of another futile project. Most of these projects are well intended, and many are well designed from a technical perspective. The most frequently omitted element is a passionate and widespread sense of ownership, from senior managers and from front-line employees. This lack of ownership is rarely expressed, but usually felt. Without the commitment of ownership, no life is breathed into an initiative. It dies a quiet death, as soon as people can safely stop paying attention to it.

As a result, we see a long parade of improvement initiatives that don't improve things. Mostly, they do little more than keep people busy for a while. Often these initiatives come at significant cost to the organization, in terms of dollars and in terms of lost good will from employees. No wonder people are skeptical of these flavors of the month! Yet most people want to improve things. Most people want to make a difference.

*looking good* is as important as results, and where results within one's area of authority are stressed over the success of the organization as a whole. A telltale sign of such organizations is the prevalence of detailed job descriptions which focus on describing activities and defining territory, rather than focusing on organization-wide meaningful results. Activity-based thinking leads to a short-term, internal focus, rather than a

## Leadership Strategies for Building Commitment to Accountability

1. Employees must be highly involved in the process, and have significant influence over the content of their own Accountability Agreements. This goes beyond informing and allowing input. This means employees have a say in what they're doing, why they're doing it, how they go about it, and what the end results look like. Sit down with people, face to face, and develop these agreements *with* them, not *for* them. Take time to study this book together. Discuss the merits and the shadow side of accountability. Listen to their hopes and concerns, and adapt this tool to their unique needs. Far more important than writing these agreements in any particular style is the deep sense of respect you can offer employees by developing these agreements flexibly and together. A high-involvement process forms the foundation for ownership and commitment to results.

2. Employees need to see commitment to accountability demonstrated at the top of the organization. Senior managers must become models for the effective use of Accountability Agreements. Employees don't need to see perfection, but they do need to see meaningful results.

3. Consequences to employees, based on results achieved, must be articulated. These must be seen as significant and likely to occur.

4. Skills are needed, both to develop an Accountability Agreement and to perform on the job. Ensure that you are providing the training and opportunities which employees require to obtain meaningful results.

5. Be certain that the results outlined in Accountability Agreements are *necessary* for the long-term success of the organization. Nothing diminishes commitment more than a sense of futility. Too often, new programs and processes turn into directives that give people more *chores* to do, as opposed to more ways to contribute meaningfully. Employees need to make a difference. Most of what is labeled a morale problem, characterized by apathy or lack of motivation, actually stems from employees not feeling useful. In every organization there will be chores, and not every goal will tap into our gifts. However, commitment to Accountability Agreements will increase to the extent that people are being encouraged to use their unique abilities, thereby fostering a sense of contribution.

> **Leadership Strategies for Building Commitment to Accountability**
>
> 6. Nurture a sense of choice, a feeling that people have significant influence over the future. Create a safe place for people to say things like "I don't know," "I don't agree," and "I need..." This will mean investing time in relationships where employees feel supported and understood. Decrease the amount of time and energy you spend *directing* employees, and increase the amount of time you spend in dialogue, encouragement, and celebration.

focus on what is best for the customer, for employees, and for the long-term success of the organization.

Organizations or groups that embrace the concept of accountability, enact Accountability Agreements, and use these agreements in a meaningful way, aren't perfect. However, they do understand that customer satisfaction and employee commitment are critical. Their focus is not on managerial power and departmental kingdoms, but rather it is on customers, employees and shareholders (all three constituencies are important). Rules in these organizations are clear, focused, and flexible. Decision making is located where the expertise and knowledge lies (where the work is performed), rather than where the pay-grade is appropriate. Employees are able to use judgment and discretion on the job. People are held accountable for results. Provided they operate in an ethical, safe, and legal manner, how they achieve those results is up to them.

## The Third Essential Leadership Quality:
Leaders learn, and help others learn, from mistakes.

Aproject manager approves an inventory control system. Months later, in spite of considerable cost and effort, the system is performing poorly. Faced with the choice of continuing to patch up and limp along with a poorly performing system, or to admit a mistake, scrap the existing system, and begin anew, the project manager opts for the latter. It's a courageous choice, because it's admitting a mistake. However, a great deal has been learned, and these learnings will be incorporated into the development of a new inventory control system. Needless to say, there is grumbling in the ranks. Employees expected a perfect system the first time around, and there is little patience for what is perceived as failure. The project manager takes the heat, but in the end it proves to be the right choice. Today, the new system is working well, and what employees originally labeled as a mistake is now understood to be simply part of the learning curve.

Somewhere, perhaps in childhood, people often pick up the notion that punishing mistakes is the best way to ensure they won't be repeated. (At least, the idea of mistakes-as-learning-opportunities was never much in evidence in the neighborhoods we grew up in. Blaming and punishing were the norm.) The legacy of blaming and punishing in organizations, however, is that most mistakes get swept under the rug. Unlike the project manager in the example above, the fear of being blamed prevents many managers from making the right decision. Instead of taking decisive action to remedy a problem, they sanction all criticism; deny, downplay, or ignore their own suspicions; and limp along with the consequences of a bad choice. In the short term, they are saved from having to admit a mistake. In the long run, the organization suffers.

Protecting an image of perfection generates enormous stress among managers and those who aspire to become managers. It becomes part of a destructive unwritten code where mistakes, instead of being acknowledged and discussed, are officially considered never to have happened. Rationalization, rather than continuous learning, is the practiced skill. Over time, younger

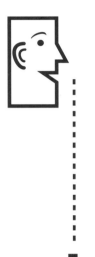

*Learning happens as a social activity, as a connection to other minds. It begins when somebody says something like, "I don't know," "I'm not sure," or "I could use some advice."*

employees catch on. Wanting to fit in and be considered for promotion, they perpetuate this selective blindness. Counterproductive though it may be, selective blindness becomes an essential ingredient of management potential. The accountability of leaders is to take the courageous step of breaking this mold, by demonstrating both humility and honesty: the humility to acknowledge their own efforts to learn and grow, and the honesty to admit the inevitable mistakes.

Accountability Agreements work well in organizations that support risk-taking, and encourage learning from rather than punishing mistakes (particularly mistakes resulting from well-intentioned initiative as opposed to carelessness). Organizations that are highly risk-averse, and that punish employees for well-intentioned mistakes, will find only limited value in this tool.

## The Fourth Essential Leadership Quality:
## Leaders encourage and challenge, they don't over-control.

SOME managers are more focused on controlling others, protecting turf, and ensuring the short-term success of their own departments than they are on customer needs, employee commitment, and the long-term success of their organizations. Even today, many systems and organizational cultures support and reward the command-and-control style of management (including classification systems, performance management systems, compensation systems, and cultural taboos against speaking up, whistle-blowing, and going over your boss's head). In such a bureaucratic, insular environment, Accountability Agreements are likely to become just one more piece of paper the boss wants filled out.

Accountability Agreements require an atmosphere of mutual trust and respect, concern for people, and interest in results. This, in turn, requires a mature and skilled workforce

■

*The essence of leadership—the ability to declare a position on an issue but remain open to influence.*

**Senge et al.**

■

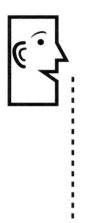

of independent and interdependent people, as opposed to employees who are so dependent they are afraid to challenge, or so counter-dependent they mindlessly resist everything the boss suggests. Accountability Agreements will greatly enhance a mature, results-oriented, people-oriented culture, but on their own they won't be enough to create such a culture. Accountability Agreements are a terrific tool, but they aren't a cure for poor leadership or deeply entrenched bureaucratic myopia.

A self-fulfilling prophecy is often at play in organizations when it comes to latitude for decision-making. If people are treated as if their abilities are suspect, they will in turn lose faith in themselves and seek an increasing amount of permission and validation. When this happens, managers—if they don't personally fall victim to self-doubt as well—will find themselves the only people capable of making decisions and bringing forth new ideas.

*Leaders count on the intelligence and integrity of the people who work with and for them.*

For Accountability Agreements to be of significant value to organizations, employees need to have elbow-room for decision making. This means leaders must have confidence in the intelligence of the people they hire. If the organization is staffed with capable people who know their jobs, the role of leaders is to encourage, challenge, and stay out of the way.

## The Fifth Essential Leadership Quality:
## Leaders reward courage, not caution.

DAVE'S daughter Mellissa wanted to play on her school basketball team, but was hesitant to approach the coach. "Why not try out?" her dad asked. "I might not be good enough," was the response. Mellissa wanted to feel confident (in her ability), fostering courage (to take the step of trying out). We often think that some measure of confidence in our

## The Moral Aspects of Leadership

The notion of accountability, and this tool that we call the Accountability Agreement, supports the four goals of moral leadership (as discussed by Gardner, 1987).

First, accountability *releases human potential* by helping people define and focus their contribution within an organization. Individuals are encouraged to exercise personal judgment and take ownership of results.

Second, the Accountability Agreement *balances the needs of the individual and the organization* with its explicit emphasis on the fair deal. Promises are made to the organization in the form of specific accountabilities, and to the individual in the form of supports and consequences.

Third, the key principles of accountability build and support results-oriented, ethical, and enlightened leadership. These are surely *essential values for organizational success* in today's knowledge-based, globally-focused workplace.

Finally, accountability requires *individual initiative*. The personal challenge inherent in this process demands the best from individuals and from their leaders. Simply put, accountability builds character.

ability precedes the courage to act. In truth, courage enables action, and action fosters confidence. Courage is thus a prerequisite to confidence, not the other way around.

You may need to stand alone to introduce Accountability Agreements in your organization. This will take courage. When you begin to talk about and practice a tool that holds people accountable, don't expect everyone to jump to your support! In some organizations, there's a huge investment in the culture of complaint, in getting by without being held accountable. To yield practical and meaningful results, Accountability Agreements require personal commitment and a high level of maturity. As such, they are unlikely to hold appeal where people have a deeply entrenched history of feeling and acting like victims, or where people are allowed to spend most of their

*If people aren't allowed room to fail, then neither will they find room to grow.*

time complaining, as opposed to claiming their own power and taking action.

Consider the following comparison of the victim mindset with the courageous mindset. Organizations which nurture the former will have difficulty with anything new, accountability most certainly included.

### The Victim Mindset

- Blames and complains.
- Carries high expectations and dependence on others, especially for direction but also for recognition, approval, and security.
- Approaches relationships and problems by dwelling on the past.
- Is self-absorbed and can only see the world through his own needs.
- Contaminates the working environment with negative feelings.
- Gossips behind people's backs.
- Fears change of any kind, and invests in resisting at all costs.
- Demonstrates no flexibility or limits, saying "yes" to everything or "no" to everything.

### The Courageous Mindset

- Owns his part of the problem, discovers opportunities to contribute, and sees himself as being in a position of choice.
- Creates her own vision and holds herself accountable for making it happen, knowing that personal security comes from within.
- Holds a realistic understanding of the past, and approaches relationships and problems primarily from the present, and with the future in mind.
- Demonstrates commitment to the greater whole and takes time for others.
- Holds himself accountable for dealing with his feelings and for being constructive.
- Communicates openly and directly, and is able to let go of resentments.
- Is willing to look at each change on its own merits, even if that change is fearful and uncertain.
- Holds a clear personal vision, maintains respect for herself and others, and can balance the needs of the organization, and of others, with her own.

# The Accountability Agreement Template  6

ACCOUNTABILITY Agreements include seven elements. Each of these elements will be described in detail in the pages which follow. If you haven't already done so, you may want to scan the real life examples at the end of this book before you read further. The examples illustrate the use of this template to build Accountability Agreements in various organizational settings.

## 1) Business Focus Statement

WHAT business-within-the-business are you in? What is your purpose or exchange with the world? What products and/or services do you provide to customers or clients within your organization? What is your unique contribution?

## 2) Accountabilities

WHAT are your job accountabilities? What outcomes or results, both specific to you and generic to similar jobs within your organization, do you promise to achieve? What is your end of the fair deal?

## 3) Supports

WHAT support do you require to fulfill your accountabilities? What resources do you need? What do you expect from managers, peers, subordinates, and others?

## 4) Measures

HOW many different ways can you think of to measure or assess your success, with respect to each of your accountabilities? What will be the indicators that you are achieving, or not achieving, your results?

## 5) Goals

WHAT are the specific, measurable, or observable results that you will commit to achieve in a given time period, within your area of accountability?

## 6) Consequences

WHAT are the personal, negotiated consequences which you will experience, based on the results you have achieved? What can you expect to happen if you achieve your results? What can you expect to happen if you don't?

## 7) Evergreen Plan

HOW will your Accountability Agreement be maintained as a significant, relevant, and flexible agreement over time?

# Where and How to Begin

## Option 1:
## Where possible, start at the top.

WHETHER you're installing Accountability Agreements for an entire company, a department, or a given work-group, the process works best if you're able to start with the top manager or leader. The leader's Accountability Agreement sets the tone, models the format, and guides the process at lower levels.

Accountability Agreements can then be implemented, one level at a time, right through to the front lines in any organization. Once a good first draft of the leader's Accountability Agreement has been completed, every one of his or her direct reports can complete a draft of their own Accountability Agreements. The leader and direct reports then meet as a group to review each person's agreement, one at a time. This process further develops individual agreements, enhances understanding of roles and interdependencies within the group, provides an opportunity to sort out shared accountabilities, and creates a check to ensure no key accountabilities have been missed or omitted.

Once strong second drafts have been completed for all members of the top management group, it's time to expand the circle of involvement. Additional input can be gathered from people who were not involved in completing the original drafts, perhaps subordinates, peers, or customers. Those providing feedback may be asked to challenge, add, delete, reword, and so on. Over a period of time, you may thus do three drafts before your Accountability Agreement is finished.

Throughout, the process needs to be flexible, involving, and open to scrutiny.

## Option 2:
## To build momentum, start with winners.

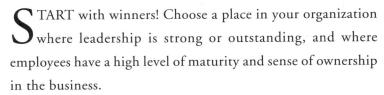

START with winners! Choose a place in your organization where leadership is strong or outstanding, and where employees have a high level of maturity and sense of ownership in the business.

Meet with the senior person or senior team in the chosen work area. Discuss accountability, its benefits, and its limitations. Share copies of this book, and meet again to discuss accountability further. Then move quickly to help the top manager in this group develop his or her Accountability Agreement. This will serve as a model for others in the work area. Follow up frequently during the initial stages of this work to provide support, to facilitate, and to advance the process. Help the group keep track of successes, and make these visible within the organization.

*Accountability Agreements are intended to be public documents within your organization. The more people who see them, the better.*

Let other groups in your organization know that you or someone else, perhaps an internal or external consultant, is available to help them develop Accountability Agreements. Initially, work only where you feel fairly confident that success is possible. Leave the difficult work-groups for a later time, when accountability will have its own momentum, and may even have become part of your organization's culture.

The most difficult part of this entire process is just getting started. Often, people delay, with endless discussions regarding the finer philosophical points of accountability, responsibility, and consequences. We urge you not to be distracted by such red herrings. If only one credible manager within your organization is willing to give this approach an honest try, you will see benefits that will encourage others. As Russell Ackoff is fond of saying, "A good idea sells itself." You don't necessarily have to start at the top of the organization, or have a large number of people initiate the approach. Start small and broadcast early results; getting people's attention and showing that accountability works will create momentum.

## Option 3:
## You always have the choice to start with yourself.

D EVELOP your own Accountability Agreement to get a feel for the power and value of this tool. Accountability Agreements have the potential to build character in your organization's culture, and perhaps even more importantly, they can help build character in people. Accountability Agreements, after all, call us to act and interact with integrity. They call us to put our often over-used slogans and rhetoric into action. They demand that we follow through on our promises and take accountability for our actions.

Use this checklist to assess your personal readiness to work with Accountability Agreements:

- Am I willing to risk trying something new? What sacrifices am I prepared to make in order to be accountable, and to ask others to be accountable?
- Have I integrated the concept of accountability with my role in the organization? Do I accept accountability for my own choices? Do I follow through on my agreements and hold myself accountable?
- How flexible am I when dealing with others? How much feedback have I solicited lately about my department's service, my professional effectiveness, and my interpersonal skills?

*Keep Accountability Agreements clear, concise, and focused on results for your customers.*

■ What are my strengths as a leader? What are my limitations?

■ What are my strengths as an entrepreneur? How well do I know my business-within-the-business? What do I contribute to the organization?

■ Do I demonstrate personal integrity? Do I make promises and keep them?

## Moving past the preliminaries:
## When it's time to start writing.

WHEN you are ready to sit down and write a strong first draft of your own Accountability Agreement, be prepared to spend two or three hours. You will be most effective if you can involve a couple of people who are familiar with your role, understand your goals, and have the willingness to invest energy in working with you (your boss, a colleague, or perhaps a subordinate). Bring along any available documentation which describes your role (old job descriptions, core competency profiles, and the like), or statements of your department's purpose, goals, and strategies; these may be helpful as reference materials. Ask participants to read this book before the meeting, then take a few minutes before you begin writing to discuss the philosophy and principles of accountability.

*Part of the art of successful living (and working) depends on learning to make and keep your agreements.*

**Hendricks & Ludeman**

Arrange for a room where the group can work without interruption. A couple of flip charts will be necessary, as well as some wall space to post flip-chart pages. (An electronic white board works even better because you will find it necessary to rewrite and reorder statements as you proceed.)

Keep in mind that this is an iterative rather than a linear process. You'll find yourself working on your business focus statement, then working on your specific accountabilities, then you get an idea for a measure or goal, then back to your business focus statement, and so on.

Begin by brainstorming the results expected from the role in question. Use the following questions to guide your working session:

- Why does your organization exist: your business, your role, your work group, your department?
- What is the scope of your individual accountability?
- What support do you need to be successful?
- What goals are you specifically accountable for within a defined period of time?
- What consequences are appropriate for positive and negative performance?
- What impediments exist that may keep you from being fully accountable for the results described, and how will you remove these?
- How often should you update this agreement?

## The joy (and the frustration) of language.

THE best Accountability Agreements are expressed in carefully chosen words. A facilitator can be helpful because clarity and conciseness are important. As with anything, you don't have to say much if you say it well. Although a discussion about how to phrase a specific accountability may feel like time wasted on word-smithing, these discussions often lead to significant new insights about expected outcomes. Struggle for the right phrasing. Tease out ineffable and overly generalized thoughts. If you can't clearly and fully describe a specific outcome, you need to push your thinking and language further. Remember, the key is to think in terms of *results* for (internal or external) customers, not *activities* to be performed.

Work at keeping accountability descriptions as brief and broad as possible. The trick is to define accountabilities at just the right level so that they provide clear direction and are meaningful to stakeholders. Describe the highest level result you want to accomplish for each area of your business or role. The lower level results are thus assumed. Avoid a paper build-up by keeping Accountability Agreements concise but deceptively powerful. Accountability statements can be like a set of nested mixing bowls. When you pick up the biggest bowl, the smaller bowls are contained within. So it is with this process; a well-written accountability statement will imply and contain the lower level accountabilities within. (Thanks to John Carver for this practical, visual analogy.)

Keep your statements brief and elegant. Minimize the use of stale evaluative words, such as maximize, optimize, effective, efficient, excellent, and the like. Avoid *helping* and *efforting* words which don't express results, for example assisting, facilitating, enabling, enhancing, or supporting.

Compare these two statements of accountability:

1.  I am personally accountable for making sure that my direct reports work effectively as a team, meet production quotas, and continue to develop their capabilities to maximize their potential and their contribution to the organization in both the long and the short term. *Or...*

2. I am personally accountable for the success of my direct reports.

The second statement is the larger mixing bowl. All the cumbersome details of the first statement are implied in the second, which is a clear expression of the desired result.

As humans, we are all inclined to be wordy when writing or talking about our work, usually because we are proud of what we do! In the human desire to be known and recognized, we share the details of our business, the variety and challenge in our activities, the power of our results. We all want customers to know everything we do for them. Yet the *details* are rarely of interest to the customer. Rather, customers want to see the *bottom line accountability*. Too many words obscure what is important. As you take each of the following seven steps, let go of old habits and fight for brevity!

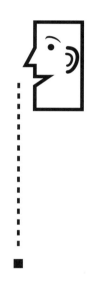

*Word-smithing leads not just to a different word, but to a different thought.*

# 8 Write an Accountability Agreement

*(You may find it helpful to refer to the Real-Life Examples section at the end of this book for many more examples of each of the following seven steps.)*

## Step One:
## Clarify Your Business Focus Statement

| Seven Steps of the Accountability Agreement |
| :---: |
| **1** |
| *Business Focus Statement* |
| **2** |
| *Accountabilities* |
| **3** |
| *Supports* |
| **4** |
| *Measures* |
| **5** |
| *Goals* |
| **6** |
| *Consequences* |
| **7** |
| *Evergreen Plan* |

THIS step requires that you describe what business you are in, the purpose of your business, and the products and services you provide to your customers. As much as possible, your business focus statement should be *unique to you and your role*. Think in terms of being in business for yourself within your organization. That is, even though you may be employed in a large company, consider yourself as a contractor or consultant to that organization—someone who has skills and talents the organization needs for a specific purpose. This helps to clarify the fact that you are making an offer into a marketplace. It just happens that at this point one customer (your employer) is buying all of your available service.

**Some examples of business focus statements...**

*A CEO of a long-term care organization*

Provide quality care for our residents and subscribers in a way that:

■ Engages families and significant others as partners.

■ Promotes choice, dignity, and respect for clients, families, staff, and volunteers.

■ Respects the limits of affordability.

- Upholds our mission and values.
- Upholds the image of the organization in the community.
- Supports innovation in continuing care.

*A senior manager of a manufacturing facility*

Create wealth for our stakeholders by the safe, reliable, and profitable manufacturing of our product line, in an environmentally and socially responsible manner. This will be done by:

- Ensuring that the integrity of assets (physical and human) is maintained.
- Maximizing long-term production of our product line.
- Ensuring that all our activities meet regulatory requirements.
- Increasing the value of our products for our customers.

*An owner/president of a mid-sized oilfield service company*

Ensure a comprehensive, competitive, and safe service to clients in need of oil and gas drilling, completions, and remedial requirements.

- Enhance shareholder value.
- Enhance long-term employee development, well being and self worth.

# Step Two:
## Write Specific and Generic Accountabilities

TAKE a moment to be clear about the distinction between *business focus statement* and *accountabilities*. You can think of the business focus statement as being the highest level outcome for your business-within-the-business, job, or role. Although accountabilities are also described in terms of outcomes or results, they are the means to your business focus. Put another way, accountabilities are the range of outcomes or results that must be achieved for you to be successful in your business focus.

Many accountabilities will be unique to your specific business or role within the organization. Others will be more generic, and may apply to several jobs at a similar level within your company.

The key to writing accountabilities is to describe significant outcomes, *not* activities, *not* processes, and *not* personal attributes. These will be outcomes your customers recognize and value. Accountabilities begin with a phrase like, "I am personally accountable for…" Following this phrase, list each accountability as in the examples below.

**Some examples of specific accountabilities…**

*A CEO of a long-term care organization*

I am personally accountable for:

- Ensuring the organization is focused on a shared vision.
- Ensuring that Company XYZ is a place you would choose to have your own family cared for.
- Ensuring that Company XYZ is a preferred employer for staff and volunteers.
- Ensuring the financial viability of Company XYZ.
- Ensuring that Board direction is implemented.
- Ensuring name recognition of Company XYZ in the community.

*A senior manager of a manufacturing facility*

I am personally accountable for:

- A safe working environment.

- An environmentally responsible operation.
- Maintaining operating profits.
- Staying informed about issues and trends that may affect the operation.
- Ensuring long term asset protection.

**Some examples of generic accountabilities...**

Remember, by generic we mean that these accountabilities may apply to a number of people at your level throughout the organization. We sometimes refer to these as *leadership accountabilities*, in that they are common to a number of organizational leaders.

*Generic Leadership Accountabilities*

I am personally accountable for:

- Maintaining the company's image in the community.
- Successful business operations within my work area.
- The success of my direct reports.
- My own learning.
- Effective working relationships within the company, with customers, within the industry, and within the community.
- Modeling ethical practice.
- Getting feedback on my performance.
- Supporting and communicating corporate directives and initiatives.
- A work environment that fosters participation, creativity, learning, and accountability.

# Step Three:
# Make Support Agreements

At this step, you have the advantage of creating support agreements which hold your boss, peers, and others accountable to you. When it is made clear that achievement of agreed-upon results is contingent on the provision of adequate resources, you have a handshake bargain with those who can make the necessary resources available. In this sense, accountability flows up, down, and sideways in an organization.

It's important to carefully think through, and list, the essential resources and support you will need to fulfill your accountabilities, and to achieve your goals during a given time period. These should be kept at a fairly high level, so avoid the details and list only significant support requirements. Making your support requirements explicit challenges you to think through how you will accomplish each accountability.

**Some examples of support requirements...**

- Timely, accurate data from the operating committee.
- Three additional engineers on project XYZ.
- Completion of XYZ systems design by April 15th.
- LAN hook-up within the department.
- Task-force willingness to renegotiate accountabilities as circumstances change.
- Elbow-room for decision making.
- Technical advice from my superintendent.
- Continued feedback and coaching from the CEO.
- Increased funding for staff training.
- Work crews who share my goals and who take pride in their work.

■ Funding for consulting help during project XYZ start-up.

■ A boss who encourages risk-taking and who understands the odd mistake.

■ A spouse who understands my irregular time demands in emergencies.

■ One hour of my manager's time every month to discuss changing priorities.

## Step Four:
## Brainstorm a List of Measures

MEASURES are simply a brainstormed list of the ways you might assess or quantify how successful you have been in fulfilling your accountabilities. Simply put, how will you measure your results? This is the interim step between accountabilities and goals. The only purpose in generating measures is to prepare for the next step in the process, which is goal-setting. Measures make it easier to write specific goals, because once you have created measures, you know how to make your accountabilities quantifiable.

For example, the measure "lost-time accidents," might well be used in the next step to create the goal: "No lost-time accidents during this operating period." In the same way, the measure "weekly staff meetings" could be turned into a goal such as: "Hold management meetings weekly, except during plant turnaround."

Once your goals have been developed in the next step of this process, your list of measures can be set aside until the next time you revise your goals.

Some examples of measures...

■ Lost-time accidents.

■ Internal audits.

■ New contracts.

■ Exit interview data.

■ Staff turnover.

■ New initiatives undertaken/completed.

■ Improvements to services.

■ Reports or assessments completed.

■ Information sessions held.

■ Employee suggestions used.

■ Feedback from customers.

■ Customer wait lists.

■ Measures of performance against budget.

■ Observations of employees interacting.

■ Weekly staff meetings.

# Step Five:
## Define Your Goals

G OALS must be time-based and in some way measurable or observable. If you have no way of knowing whether you have achieved your goal, then it's not a goal, it's just an idea. Not all of your accountabilities will be turned into specific goals for each operating period. We recommend no more than five or six goals for any given time period. Nonetheless, you are still answerable for all of your accountabilities.

Some examples of goals...

■ Achieve a 15% return on invested capital during the 3rd quarter.

- Complete my 360° feedback this year.
- Publish two articles this year.
- Restructure the engineering department by year end.
- Complete plant turnaround by April 27th.
- No lost-time accidents this year.
- Achieve a rating of B+ or better on this year's internal audit.
- Get customer wait list down to thirty days.

## Step Six:
## Negotiate Consequences

THE process of negotiating consequences for results changes the nature of the relationship between an employer and an employee. It means people are required to take an adult perspective, and state what they want from their employer, versus the adult-child approach implicit in many employer-employee relationships. In the latter, the employee does the required job and waits to see what the organization will offer in return (an arbitrary consequence). Simply discussing consequences helps to generate an open relationship between an employee and employer. A discussion of consequences builds insight into what is personally important, hopes and fears about the future, mutual interdependence, and the need to be accountable to one another.

**Some general examples of consequences by type...**

*Positive consequences:*
- Praise, recognition.
- Rewards such as an increase in salary, a bonus, or an extra week of vacation.
- Reduced personal stress.

## Writing Goal Statements

The secret to writing clear goals is to separate logical levels or types of information. Otherwise it's too easy to get bogged down with long-winded, well-intentioned, obtuse goal statements. The result you're after is a clear, measurable or observable goal. The three levels of information relevant to this process are *intent*, *goal*, and *action plan*. Only write as much in intent and action plan as you need to in order to get clarity about the specific goal.

Your intent statement may include all the flowery and evaluative words you can think of; maximize, facilitate, optimize, finalize, effectively, and address all fit in this category. "To effectively address and optimize the value we receive from product XYZ" is a statement of intent. It is totally meaningless as a goal, but it does convey a sense of your direction.

Parallel to this statement of intent, write your goal statement. Keep this simple (a sentence at most), and it *must* be measurable or observable, as in, "complete project XYZ report by March 16th," or "have project XYZ report approved by the Board by January 17th." This is by far the hardest of the three levels to write well. Don't use any evaluative words, not one "effectively" or "efficiently!" It's tough, so just do a first draft. You can come back and clean it up later. You'll also find that your goals (if they're measurable or in some way observable) are at best only an approximation of what you really intend. This is normal. As a result, you may need more than one goal to address the same intent statement.

As you write your intent and goal statements, a hodge-podge of ideas for achieving these comes rushing out at you. Don't lose these thoughts. Note them under action plans. This information can be used later to help you organize *how* to accomplish your goals. Don't worry about the priority, order, or clarity of these ideas at this time. For now, action plans is just a catch-all or data-dump for everything that is not an intent or goal. This includes things like sequencing, scheduling, steps, milestones, resources needed, who needs to be involved, assumptions, time demands, and so on.

- Enjoyable work relationships.
- Feelings such as a sense of satisfaction and achievement.
- An increase in budget allocation.
- An opportunity to demonstrate competence.

*Negative consequences:*

- An unsatisfactory but fair performance evaluation.
- Less freedom for decision making, closer supervision for a period of time.
- Loss of a privilege.
- Decrease in, or loss of an annual bonus.
- No salary increase.

*Punitive consequences:*

*(As stated earlier, punitive consequences are **not** the focus of Accountability Agreements. These examples are provided for comparison purposes only.)*

- Progressive discipline process, disciplinary action such as a letter of warning.
- A decrease in salary.
- Demotion to a lower level.
- Layoff or firing.

**Some examples of specific consequences…**

*Consequences involving a direct dollar cost:*

- I will be granted 1000 units in the company's Employee Stock Ownership Program.
- I will receive a salary increase equivalent to the top 5% of employees.
- I will be funded to attend one international conference next year.

*Consequences not involving a direct dollar cost:*

■ Through making these contributions I will be promoted to general manager within 5 years.

■ Through making these contributions I will receive an acceptable performance rating and be granted the trust and flexibility I need to work independently.

■ I will receive recognition and appreciation from the company and from clients.

*Consequences that are intangible and intrinsic:*

■ A sense of satisfaction and pride in having met a considerable challenge and performed well.

■ Improved confidence in my ability to help clients achieve meaningful business results.

■ Enjoyment of the work itself, and of the trust and confidence customers place in me.

# Step Seven:
## Evergreen Plan

AN Accountability Agreement should gather no dust! Keep yours close at hand. Use it as a guide to both long-term and day-to-day decision making. Remember, it is your day-to-day decisions that determine, over time, not just the nature and direction of your business but ultimately the level of your success.

Now that you have completed your Agreement, plan to keep it alive and flexible. Have an agreed-upon review time so it doesn't join those other planning documents that grow moldy in office filing cabinets. Renewing your Accountability Agreement need not be onerous, but without the discipline of regular monitoring, the opportunity offered by accountability is easily lost.

**Some examples of the evergreen plan...**

- Review Accountability Agreements quarterly within the work group.
- Make changes as appropriate within one week of each review meeting.
- Keep my Accountability Agreement in my day-timer for regular review.

# 9 A Learning Process

IDEALLY, accountability begins with the CEO and senior management team and slowly develops from there, gradually building experience, confidence, and success. The process can also start with a particularly keen or innovative team, while others watch for results. The principles can be introduced through human-resource professionals, building a shift in attitude one person or department at a time. However these ideas move in an organization, there will be some person or group of people who champion the concepts and keep them moving. Someone needs to be accountable for accountability.

Those who are accountable for the development of accountability will need a high level of self-awareness and commitment to self-reflection. Some of the questions which must be asked regularly are:

- What are we learning as we implement these ideas? How are we recording our learning?
- What results are we seeing? What results are we expecting?
- Are we broadcasting successes? Sharing insights? Clarifying our thinking?
- Have we reverted back to less useful assumptions about people, organizational culture, or the nature of accountability?
- Have we defined what we each mean by accountability?
- What does our learning tell us about the next step in this evolution?
- Are we *adapting* and tailoring these tools and concepts to our organization, or simply *adopting* them blindly?

■ Are we experiencing any elements of the shadow side of accountability? Are we intimidating rather than empowering? How can we counteract these tendencies?

■ How much effort is required to maintain our process? How can we streamline?

■ How do we measure our success with this tool? Are our profits up? Are our costs down? Are people making better decisions? Are people following through on their commitments? Are we contributing in ways which are measurable and meaningful to the organization? Is there more energy and enthusiasm?

The writing of good Accountability Agreements requires skills which can be developed. Setting realistic goals, asking for the necessary supports, negotiating meaningful consequences—all these are skills which can be learned and improved. Invest in people's development in these areas. Support them and help them make this work.

Expect a continuing shift in corporate culture, not all of which will be comfortable. Accountability opens the door to honest communication, including open disagreement. People become more vocal. Front-line staff may challenge their results expected versus supports received. Employees will anticipate some room to negotiate consequences. People will begin to hold one another accountable. Over time, the dynamics in management relationships shift from parent/child to adult/adult. This will feel unfamiliar at first. Nostalgia—for that which never was—may emerge. These are growing pains, but they are accompanied by great rewards.

Embrace the stance of the learning organization. Experiential learning is essentially three things: *doing, reflecting,* and *recreating. Doing* alone is not enough to build learning.

*Reflecting* and *recreating* are crucial. Then the cycle begins again: more doing, enhanced by all that has been learned. A conscious, self-aware process builds change which will last.

# Moving into Action 10

AS with anything new, the hardest part is getting started. We all learn by doing. Your appreciation for the depth and power of accountability, and Accountability Agreements, will grow only as you begin to apply these ideas. The best possible advice we can give you at this point is to give this process a try.

In our experience, a kind of magic happens when you complete your own Accountability Agreement. The process facilitates a completely new kind of conversation between people inside organizations. We have had clients tell us that writing their own Agreements helped them understand—often for the first time—what contribution they were making to their organizations. People gain clarity about their commitments, their results, their consequences, their *fair deal*. Understanding what fair deal you are operating under is profoundly empowering. Writing your Accountability Agreement will build that knowledge.

In this book, we have offered the promise of accountability. It is now your option to take that promise to results. Remember that help is available if you choose, and that help may be a good idea, particularly if building a culture of accountability is going to be a stretch for your organization. We welcome the opportunity to work with this tool in organizations; contact numbers are available at the back of this book if you wish to reach any of the authors. We encourage you to seek out accountable people to work with you.

Accountability builds results. It builds stronger leaders, more successful employees, and thriving organizations. We challenge you to put this tool to work, and invite you to watch for and prosper from the results accountability brings.

# Real-Life Examples

ACCOUNTABILITY Agreements have been used with great results in a wide variety of organizations. The following examples demonstrate the use of this tool in large corporations and entrepreneurial partnerships, with line management and in support roles, with teachers, lawyers, financial planners, and sales people. Each example is adapted from a real-life application (all specific identifying details have, of course, been changed).

Note the differences in writing styles, and the flexibility available in tailoring Accountability Agreements to meet the needs of your unique situation. Use all seven elements of the tool, but adapt those elements to the culture of your organization.

- **Example 1**: An Accountability Agreement for the CEO of a Pharmaceutical Research Company, p. 78.
- **Example 2**: An Accountability Agreement for the Operations Manager of a Major Petroleum Producer, p. 80.
- **Example 3**: An Accountability Agreement for the Physical Plant Department Management Team of a Major University, p. 82.
- **Example 4**: An Accountability Agreement for the Support Services Manager of a Major Insurance Company, p. 84.
- **Example 5**: An Accountability Agreement for an External Management Consultant (Co-author Bruce Klatt), p. 86.

- **Example 6**: An Accountability Agreement for the Supervisor of Network Services of a Major Corporation, p. 88.

- **Example 7**: An Accountability Agreement for a Secondary School Teacher, p. 90.

- **Example 8**: An Accountability Agreement for an Entrepreneurial Publishing Company (Our Publisher, RedStone), p. 92.

- **Example 9**: An Accountability Agreement for a Human Resources Advisor, p. 94.

- **Example 10**: An Accountability Agreement for the Managing Partner in a Financial Services Firm, p. 96.

- **Example 11**: An Accountability Agreement for a Sales Agent, p. 98.

- **Example 12**: An Accountability Agreement for a Partner/Group Leader in a Law Firm, p. 100.

- **Example 13**: An Accountability Agreement for an Entrepreneurial Coaching Firm, p. 102.

- **Example 14**: An Accountability Agreement for the Executive Director of Public Relations in a Community-Supported Organization, p. 104.

- **Example 15**: An Accountability Agreement for a Young Adult Job-Seeker, p. 106.

- **Example 16**: An Accountability Agreement for a Professional Strategic Alliance, p. 108.

**Example 1:**
An Accountability Agreement for the CEO of a Pharmaceutical Research Company

## Business Focus Statement
- Ensure the safety, efficacy, and availability of all products.
- Maximize long-term growth and success through new product development and diversification.
- Maximize shareholder value and corporate profitability.

## Accountabilities
*I am personally accountable for:*
- The success of my direct reports and through them the success of the company.
- Influencing, interpreting and implementing the policies of the Board of Directors.
- Development, understanding, and implementation of long-term corporate strategy.
- Ensuring that we are perceived by public and private stakeholders in a positive manner.
- Ensuring finances are sufficient to achieve present and future goals.
- Exercising leadership and developing an organization that is capable of learning and adapting quickly to change.
- My own development as a leader and CEO.
- Ensuring the safety of our products and employees, and the fulfillment of our regulatory obligations.
- Minimizing the financial and legal liability of Directors.

## Supports
- Direct reports to define and fulfill accountabilities and goals.
- Direct reports and managers to work effectively as a team throughout the organization.
- Direct reports to provide leadership, enabling a productive and flexible organization.
- Board of Directors to approve and support public offering, annual budget and goals, compensation and rewards.

## Measures
- Public image as measured by press releases.
- Stock price increases.
- Perception by analysts and their reviews.
- Public offering within the next two years.

- New out-licensing agreements.
- Implementing Directors' policies.
- Evaluation of corporate and CEO's performance by Directors.
- Achieving sales increases and meeting targets.
- Development of new products.
- Innovations from research and development.

## Goals

- Share offering of $250 million by January.
- Four meetings with investment analysts per half year.
- Directors complete evaluation on my and corporate performance by August.
- Pass all regulatory inspections.
- Share price to $20 by January.
- Initiate pre-clinical work on new biotech product next year.
- Finish eight clinical trials in fiscal year.

## Consequences

- Short-term incentive program for me and my staff.
- Bonus arrangement as negotiated with the Board.

## Evergreen Plan

*I will monitor my accountabilities at:*

- Weekly management meetings.
- Quarterly strategic meetings for review and development of strategies.
- Board of Director meetings.

**Example 2:**
An Accountability Agreement for the Operations Manager of a Major Petroleum Producer

*(Notice the adaptation of the business focus statement to reflect this manager's understanding of his business-within-the-business.)*

## Business Focus Statement
*Scope of My Job*
- My job encompasses all aspects of the production of oil and gas.

*Purpose of My Job*
- Maximizing the production from our production facilities.

*My Customers*
- The senior management team.
- The production supervisors.

*My Products*
- Employees with the skills required to produce oil and gas efficiently and safely.
- Plant facilities which can operate at capacity.
- Oil and gas delivered to the pipeline.

## Accountabilities
*I am personally accountable for:*
- Meeting or exceeding our targets for oil and gas volumes delivered to the pipeline.
- Keeping our unit costs at or below estimates.
- Positive working relationships with the communities in which our plants operate.
- Harmonious working relationships with the union.
- Skill levels of operating personnel.
- Operating safety.

## Supports
- Goodwill and respect for bargaining process from union leaders.
- Continued commitment from senior management team to employee training budget.
- Continued commitment to excellence from employees.

## Measures
- Production per quarter.
- Number of safety incidents.
- Equipment down-time rate.

- Employee acquisition of new skills.
- Communities survey results.

## Goals

- Team trained to conduct industry educational presentations in local schools.
- Production levels for the quarter at 5% over same quarter last year.
- Establish bargaining process with union representatives for coming round of negotiations.

## Consequences

- I will be promoted to general manager within five years.
- I will be funded to attend the international petroleum show in Houston next year.
- I will be granted 1000 units in the company's Employee Stock Ownership Program.
- I will receive a salary increase equivalent to the top 5% of employees.

## Evergreen Plan

- Review Accountability Agreement with peers and senior management team annually.
- Review accountabilities as part of weekly planning activity.

## Example 3:
## An Accountability Agreement for the Physical Plant Department Management Team of a Major University

*(Notice the unique use of this tool with a team rather than an individual. This is only possible in a genuine team setting, where members of the team experience a strong sense of shared fate. For one to succeed, all must succeed. This is much rarer in organizations than one might think. Notice also the useful separation between negotiated and natural consequences in this example.)*

## Business Focus Statement
■ Ensure campus infrastructure meets the needs of the university community.

## Accountabilities
*We are personally accountable for:*
■ A world-class university facility (inviting, clean, easy to navigate, functional, reliable).
■ Customer satisfaction with our service and cost.
■ Ensuring compliance with all government and university policies.
■ Meeting the ongoing maintenance and future infrastructure needs of the campus.
■ Ensuring the finance office has the information they require about physical plant operations.
■ A department capable of learning and adapting quickly to change.
■ Our own development as team leaders.
■ The success of our direct reports.
■ Working within budget and allocating resources wisely.
■ Developing and maintaining positive working relationships.
■ Staying abreast of the latest trends, technologies, and issues.

## Supports
■ Direct reports work effectively as a team.
■ Senior management keeps us informed on a timely basis and advocates on our behalf.
■ Campus community involves us in early stages of planning.
■ Consultants, contractors, and suppliers provide their best value.

## Measures
■ Rating on faculty and student survey.
■ Number of complaints received.

- Productive time lost due to equipment failures.
- Rating on facility comparison to other universities and colleges.

## Goals

- Rank in the top ten of excellently-maintained university facilities next year.
- Decrease number of complaints received by 10% from last year.
- Gain senior management approval for our five-year facility plan by January.

## Negotiated Consequences

- We will be considered for promotional opportunities as they arise.
- Each team member will receive a minimum of one funded site visit annually to study leading physical plant operations throughout North America.
- We will become a pilot case in tying salary increases to performance.

## Natural Consequences

- Others benchmark against our operations.
- We are invited to speak at conferences.
- Other university departments are given the opportunity for team management.

## Evergreen Plan

- Review Accountability Agreement with this team every three months.

**Example 4:**

## An Accountability Agreement for the Support Services Manager of a Major Insurance Company

*(Notice the various types of support required to fulfill the accountabilities in this position. Be specific about what you need, and who you need it from.)*

### Business Focus Statement
■ Meet all administrative, support staff, and facilities management needs within the company.

### Accountabilities
*I am personally accountable for:*
■ Client satisfaction.
■ Ensuring a clear and communicated strategic direction for support services.
■ Ensuring that all management team members and employees have the equipment, information, and training necessary to do their jobs.
■ My own development.
■ Ensuring that policies, rules, and regulations of the company, and provincial and federal laws are not violated.
■ Ensuring a safe, healthy, and productive work environment.
■ Effective and clearly-defined working relationships with employees, clients, and external suppliers.
■ Ensuring that job applicants have a good impression of our company.
■ Developing the overall production capacity within support services.

### Supports
*From the Director*
■ Monthly meetings to review my progress and provide specific feedback.
■ Help removing roadblocks which arise.
■ Appropriate budget for the necessary technology upgrades.
*From staff*
■ Competent, productive staff who work well together and with clients.
*From clients*
■ Honest, timely communication about any areas of dissatisfaction.

### Measures
■ File processing time.
■ Complaints from clients, both internal and external.
■ Staff turnover.
■ Sanctions for non-compliance with regulators.

## Goals

- Gain budget approval and create agenda for staff development day to be held this fall.
- Complete audit of computer system capabilities this summer.
- Establish single-point-of-contact system for follow-up by the end of the calendar year.

## Consequences

- Extended six-week vacation next year to take family to Europe.
- Complete discretion over hiring, firing, and compensation beginning next year.

## Evergreen Plan

- Review Accountability Agreement during my annual performance review.
- Set new goals every 90 days, using this framework.
- Solicit feedback from direct reports on my Accountability Agreement, after their annual performance reviews.

**Example 5:**

An Accountability Agreement for an External Management Consultant
(Co-author Bruce Klatt)

*(External consultants—and most internal consultants—are in the business of
supporting others to achieve their results. In that role, it is easy to lose sight of one's
own results and start writing accountabilities in terms of "helping" others. But
"helping" is not a result. Note the results language in this example.)*

## Business Focus Statement
- Ensure that clients move quickly, strategically, and honestly from problems to
  solutions in organizational design.

## Accountabilities
*I am personally accountable for:*
- Analyzing client issues from a systemic viewpoint.
- Ensuring that clients are equipped with the knowledge and tools to produce
  the results they seek.
- Identifying threats and opportunities which clients may not see.
- Creating an environment which is conducive to honest communication.
- Maintaining a position of objectivity.
- Representing myself, my services, and my colleagues honestly.
- Building and maintaining long-term relationships with clients.
- My own professional development.
- My reputation and referrability.
- Running a profitable business.

## Supports
- Honest communication from clients.
- Encouragement, shadow coaching, recommended reading, and other shared
  professional development from colleagues.
- Referrals from colleagues and clients.
- Assistance with specific tasks from my spouse during busy times.
- Critical analysis and advice from my publishers.
- Repeat business from long-term clients.

## Measures
- Number of referrals from clients and colleagues, and repeat business with clients.
- Measures of success used by clients (whatever these may be).
- Feedback from clients.
- Books and articles studied.

- New approaches tried.
- Financial profitability.
- Books and articles published.
- Presentations at conferences.

## Goals

- Study 50 new business-related books this year.
- Attend one workshop/training program as a participant every year.
- Work with three new clients this year.
- Publish two books this year.
- Speak at one conference before next summer.

## Consequences

*Positive Consequences (when I achieve my accountabilities)*

- One extraordinary holiday with my family this year.
- Expanded client base, longer-term contracts, increased income, and more options.

*Consequences of failure (if I do not achieve my accountabilities)*

- Loss of clients, declining income, less ability to select the type of work I most enjoy doing.

## Evergreen Plan

- Review my goals every quarter.
- Discuss my accountabilities with colleagues annually.

## Example 6:
An Accountability Agreement for the Supervisor of Network Services of a Major Corporation

## Business Focus Statement
- Ensure that all employees have the corporately-approved information systems that they require to do their work, and that these systems are cost-effective, current, and fully operational.

## Accountabilities
*I am personally accountable for:*
- Ensuring that user expectations are negotiated, agreed to, and incorporated into our service level agreement (SLA).
- Working within or exceeding the commitments set out in our SLA.
- Ensuring that new employees have a basic understanding of our information systems.
- Ensure the integrity of corporate data and corporate information systems.
- Ensuring that all information-systems assets are inventoried and can be accounted for at any time.
- Staying current on the latest technology.
- Ensuring compatibility with information systems in shareholder companies.
- The success of my direct reports.
- Delivering service within budget.

## Supports
- Users are trained with the skills and knowledge to use their technology effectively.
- Procurement department follows our recommendations.
- Company managers and project leaders understand and adhere to the conditions and timelines set out in the SLA.
- My manager keeps me informed of corporate issues that may affect Network Services.
- Adequate budget for Network Services employees' training and development.
- Help Desk manages and deals directly with users re day to day requests.

## Measures
- Customer request response time.
- Number of incidents which exceed SLA parameters.
- Accuracy of inventory.
- Incidents of data loss.

- Budget variance.
- Customer satisfaction/complaints.

## Goals

- Implement preventive maintenance program by end of year.
- No incidents to exceed SLA parameters in this quarter.
- Complete review of critical data protection procedures by September.
- Participate in this year's senior management team retreat, in preparation for drafting a new three-year technology plan.
- Attend two professional development opportunities this year.

## Consequences

- I will be appointed to chair the committee which writes the three-year technology plan.
- I will be given the opportunity to visit our parent company's head office to participate in further creative planning.
- I will be able to submit a credible bid for the department manager's position in two years.
- I will be recognized as an effective communicator with expertise in bridging the gap between users and technology.

## Evergreen Plan

- Post my accountabilities in my office to guide day-to-day activity.
- Review with direct reports monthly.

## Example 7:
An Accountability Agreement for a Secondary School Teacher

## Business Focus Statement
*Provide quality education in my classroom in a way that:*
- Engages my students in a stimulating, dynamic, shared learning environment.
- Respects the dignity and self-worth of everyone in the classroom.
- Upholds learning expectations as outlined by the Department of Education.
- Engages parents, students, and teachers to work together as partners.

## Accountabilities
*I am personally accountable for:*
- A safe learning environment which is creative, dynamic, and conducive to learning.
- A classroom which is passionate and energized.
- Ensuring individual learning by matching learning style with available resources.
- Recognizing and building on the strengths of students and parents.
- Ensuring that my behaviour is a reflection of my core values (honesty, accountability, choice, respect for differences, and excitement for learning).
- Ensuring fair consequences for inappropriate behaviour.
- Meeting and exceeding the basic education and contractual obligations as set out by the department and our professional association.
- Staying informed on issues and resources that may affect my classroom.
- My physical, psychological, and spiritual health.

## Supports
- Trust from my principal, and time to solicit feedback.
- Scheduled opportunities to share challenges, needs, and experiences with colleagues.
- Understanding when I say "no" to activities not directly related to my accountabilities (from my principal, peers, students, and parents).
- Parents who will respect my initiatives and communicate honestly when they do not agree.

## Measures
- Quality of contact with students: conversation, observation, verbal and non-verbal feedback.
- Test scores, assignment completions, attendance.
- Energy level in the classroom.
- Feedback from peers, administrators, and parents.

■ Personal, subjective evaluation (e.g. Am I having fun in the classroom? How is my own personal level of motivation and energy? Do I sleep well?).

## Goals

■ Discuss my Accountability Agreement in an age-appropriate way with my students during the first week of class.

■ Assess the individual needs of each student and develop individual "learning contracts" within the first three months.

■ Discuss my accountabilities with each parent when I meet with them during the first round of parent-teacher interviews.

■ Develop a better support system for myself outside the classroom by planning two outings a month with friends or colleagues.

## Consequences

■ Parents will be more aware of what I am accountable for as a teacher, what their children are accountable for as students, and what they are accountable for in the learning process.

■ Students will be more aware of their roles and accountabilities.

■ I will experience greater personal satisfaction.

■ I will benefit from increased peer support.

■ I will have the opportunity to attend one additional conference outside our school division in the last half of the year.

## Evergreen Plan

■ Review my Accountability Agreement personally every week.

■ Review my Accountability Agreement with parents during parent-teacher interviews.

■ Discuss this tool with my colleagues.

■ Solicit feedback from my principal on an ongoing basis.

■ Invite parents to give me ongoing feedback on my accountabilities.

## Example 8:
## An Accountability Agreement for an Entrepreneurial Publishing Company (Our Publisher, RedStone)

### Business Focus Statement
- We are the "self-publishing author's publisher." We create and drive products from concept to sales, including manuscript development, editing, design, packaging, marketing, and distribution.

### Accountabilities—Product Development
*We are personally accountable for:*
- Ensuring the creation of a highly marketable product that brings strong value to readers.
- Ensuring that the author's voice is reflected in the published product.
- Ensuring that a project plan is in place and that timelines are agreed to and met.
- Ensuring that the author is in agreement with the budget, and that the author's money is invested wisely.

### Accountabilities—Product Marketing
*We are personally accountable for:*
- Ensuring that the author excels at marketing his or her own published product.
- Ensuring that a marketing plan is in place, with sales targets and timelines.
- Ensuring that a publicity plan is in place that promotes exposure for the author and the product in target media.
- Ensuring maximum direct product sales to the author's client networks.
- Ensuring the broadest possible distribution of the author's product.
- Ensuring an open, accurate, and fair accounting of all proceeds.

### Supports
- Authors who are committed to the same standards of excellence and value.
- Authors who are prepared to accept our coaching on manuscript development, editing, and design.
- Authors who meet their deadlines and work within the agreed-upon plan.
- Authors who are prepared to work with our recommended suppliers.
- Authors who will follow through on their financial and other agreements.
- Authors who will accept the terms of our distribution contract.
- Authors who are willing and available to be coached as promoters, and who see themselves as both well-positioned and accountable to sell books.
- Authors who will communicate openly, honestly, and in a timely fashion.

## Measures
- Number of books sold in a given time period.
- Reader feedback on all aspects of the book.
- Number of clients making large bulk purchases of books.
- Author satisfaction with all phases of the development process.
- Author's success in acting as a book marketer.
- Media coverage generated.
- Timeliness of all phases of the development process.
- Accuracy and timeliness of record-keeping.
- Project completed on budget.
- General availability of book to the mass public.
- Successful penetration of target markets.

## Goals
- Specific goals and time periods are negotiated on a project-by-project basis.

## Consequences
*Natural consequences if we achieve our goals:*
- We will publish excellent products that generate strong revenues.
- We will have the opportunity to develop additional products with the same author.
- We will attract new publishing clients.
- We will have an excellent reputation in the publishing industry.
- We will attract new clients into other parts of our business.
- We will have the opportunity to choose our clients.

*Natural consequences if we do not achieve our goals:*
- We will lose credibility with our clients.
- We may lose the opportunity to develop future products, with current and new clients.
- Other aspects of the business may suffer as a result of lost client confidence.
- We may not be able to attract the partners we wish to work with.
- We will lose book-sales revenue and profitability.

*Specific negotiated consequences may also apply.*

## Evergreen Plan
- During the product development phase, we work closely with the author and will solicit regular feedback. During the product marketing phase, we will conduct regular meetings with the author to ensure our accountabilities are being met.

## Example 9:
## An Accountability Agreement for a Human Resources Advisor

### Business Focus Statement
- Employment systems and practices that value differences and treat people fairly.
- Leading-edge staffing practices.
- Enhanced capacity in managers to make successful staffing decisions.

### Accountabilities
*I am personally accountable for:*
1. *Staffing*
- Ensuring that staffing processes are based on core competencies, and developing assessment tools to support this framework.
- Ensuring that managers in the hiring process understand best practices, are clear on the outcomes they seek, understand applicable regulatory and policy issues, and know their accountabilities.
- Developing and creating organizational support for redeployment.
- Spending the advertising budget wisely, and ensuring consistent and effective advertising.
- Ensuring that immigration processes are met.
- Ensuring that job applicants have a good impression of our organization.
2. *Leadership*
- Coaching and mentoring the staffing team to deal with current conflict and leadership issues.
- The success of my direct reports.
- Staying abreast of the latest legislation, trends, and issues in staffing.
- Modeling ethical behaviour.
- Ensuring that department heads understand the need for human resource and succession planning.

### Supports
- Weekly meetings and prompt, frank feedback from my Director.
- Opportunity to influence decisions that affect recruitment and selection.
- Exposure to senior management on staffing issues.
- Full-time support person dedicated to staffing.
- Faster computer.
- Continued coaching from our external consultant.

### Measures
- Ratio of posting to hire time.
- Number of managers coached.

- Specific approaches used in the staffing process.
- New initiatives developed (manual, tip sheets, handbooks).
- Number of positions filled.
- Violations of policies and regulations.

## Goals

- Establish mechanism for measuring hiring-managers' satisfaction by end of quarter (including structure questionnaire, follow-up meetings).
- Conduct two coaching sessions with line managers I have not yet worked with by end of quarter.
- Review advertising effectiveness for past six months by end of quarter.

## Consequences

- Verbal and written recognition from director.
- Freedom from clerical work.
- Director represents me as promotable.
- Opportunity to attend this fall's Human Resource conference.
- Opportunity to begin further education program.
- Self-development and pride in my work and reputation.

## Evergreen Plan

- Review progress with Director once per quarter during goal-setting.
- Keep this document in my activity planner as a constant reminder.

**Example 10:**

An Accountability Agreement for the Managing Partner in a Financial Services Firm

## Business Focus Statement
- Clarify the life and financial goals of clients.
- Create a financial strategy to meet and/or exceed those goals.
- Implement that strategy.

## Accountabilities
*I am personally accountable for:*
- Ensuring the implementation of all marketing plans.
- Creating, developing, and managing our client service process.
- Ensuring regular, ongoing communication with existing clients.
- The success of our staff team.
- Ensuring that the business operates efficiently on a day-to-day basis.
- My physical, mental, emotional, and professional well-being.

*My partner and I are jointly accountable for:*
- Creating, delivering, and protecting a consistent business image.
- Creating a marketing plan consistent with our image.
- Defining and working within a profitable target market.
- Ensuring the financial health of our business.
- Open, honest, and timely partnership communication, and resolution of partnership stalemates using the advisory board where necessary.

## Supports
- My partner stays focused on generating qualified opportunities within our target markets.
- My partner provides timely feedback on all aspects of the business operation.
- All team members independently and proactively fulfill their accountabilities.
- Our clients respect and work with our client service process.

## Measures
- Total revenues and expenses.
- Annual review for every Top 100 client.
- Number of qualified referrals from clients.
- Level of staff turnover.
- Number of clients who leave.
- Client satisfaction survey results.
- Personal income levels.

## Goals

■ These will be set quarterly and communicated to all team members within three days.

## Natural Consequences

■ Potential clients will seek us out for service.
■ Our clients and strategic allies will have full confidence in referring business to us.
■ We will achieve our mission, which is to see our clients meet their goals.
■ Our incomes will go up and we will have more time off.

## Negotiated Consequences

■ 154 free days this year.
■ Three-week trip to Italy this year.
■ Bonuses for all team members.

## Evergreen Plan

■ Review this document weekly with all team members.
■ Use this document to guide quarterly goal-setting.
■ Laminate this document and keep on hand to guide decision-making and prioritize actions.

## Example 11:
## An Accountability Agreement for a Sales Agent

*(This is the Accountability Agreement for the sales agent who manages David Irvine's speaking business. Note the creative negotiated consequences used in this example. These rewards hold personal meaning and incentive for this individual.)*

### Business Focus Statement
■ Generate opportunities for my client to share his message by prospecting, promoting, and selling his speaking business and products to audiences who will benefit from what he has to offer.

### Accountabilities
*I am personally accountable for:*
1. *Prospecting*
■ Creating short- and medium-term opportunities in current markets.
■ Creating longer-term opportunities in target markets where my client's message is particularly applicable.
2. *Promoting*
■ Increasing the public profile of my client and his message.
■ Ensuring my client is prepared to make full use of promotional opportunities.
3. *Selling*
■ Closing deals for speaking engagements and product sales.
■ Generating financial success for myself and my client.
4. *Customer Service*
■ Ensuring that the audiences we work with are a good fit for my client's message.
■ Ensuring that our audiences receive the value they are seeking.

### Supports
■ My client consistently delivers value to our audiences.
■ My client spends time to ensure that I understand his message and purpose.
■ My client generates referral business from each engagement.
■ Sales training and coaching.
■ Freedom to make decisions relevant to the sales process.

### Measures
■ Audience feedback on the value received.
■ Fees earned per engagement.
■ Number of bookings in target markets.
■ Number of referrals.
■ Product sales revenue.

- Quality of communication between me and my client.
- My income level and personal satisfaction.

## Goals

- Minimum 15 prospecting calls per week for this quarter.
- Bookstore tour of local market by end of quarter.
- Twenty booked engagements this quarter.
- Client feedback survey ratings no less than 8.5 out of 10.
- Meet two new key relationships.

## Consequences

*If I achieve my goals:*

- At the end of the first quarter, I will receive a one-day spa treatment.
- At the end of the second quarter, I will receive one day's paid accommodation at a local resort.
- At the end of the third quarter, I will receive a cash advance toward a vacation.
- At the end of the fourth quarter, I will receive dinner for two and tickets to a seasonal event of my choice.
- At the end of the year, I will receive a bonus on all booked business.
- I will have earned a strong bargaining position for additional administrative support for the coming year.

*If I do not achieve my goals:*

- I will not be eligible for these rewards.
- I will not have as strong a bargaining position for my next year's contract.
- My relationship with my client may suffer.
- I will not experience as high a level of personal satisfaction.

## Evergreen Plan

- I will use this document to set quarterly goals with my client.
- I will check my progress against this document every week.

**Example 12:**
An Accountability Agreement for a Partner/Group Leader in a Law Firm

## Business Focus Statement

■ Provide understandable estate-planning solutions for our clients, designed so that our clients will achieve their individual, family, and business goals.

## Accountabilities

*I am personally accountable for:*

■ Ensuring that the group business focus statement is implemented.
■ Ensuring our practice group is focused on a shared vision.
■ Developing innovative estate-planning solutions that help our clients achieve their goals.
■ Ensuring that our products are tax-planned, understandable, and of the highest quality.
■ Ensuring that our group is profitable.
■ Ensuring name recognition of our practice group.
■ My personal development as a dynamo—someone who is always learning, growing, and expanding my skills.
■ Ensuring that all group members develop the skills necessary to carry out our mission.

## Supports

*From management:*

■ Strategic planning assistance.
■ Wills database software.
■ Accounting software for estate accounting.
■ Faith and trust.

*From other lawyers in the group:*

■ Be a dynamo—learning, growing, and expanding skills.

*From staff:*

■ Completing work on time.
■ Taking initiative and anticipating what needs to be done.
■ Following up with clients.
■ Developing ways for us all to work smarter.

## Measures

■ Increased billings.
■ Turn-around time on files.
■ Group recognition from clients, within the firm, and among other professionals.
■ Papers published.

- Attracting high-worth clients.
- Attracting more complicated or sophisticated files.

## Goals

- Keep only files which I am currently working on in my office.
- Write and present/publish one major tax-planning paper this year.
- Obtain one new file with an industry representative from each of the following institutions this year: bank, trust company, insurance company, accounting firm, brokerage.
- Develop expertise in charitable planned giving and trust taxation over the next six months.

## Consequences

*Consequences of success:*

- Recognition by management and others that we work well together.
- We get bigger and better files.
- We'll have fun!

*Consequences of failure:*

- We may lose clients.
- The firm's reputation will suffer.
- We will lose the support of management and partners.
- We simply coast.

## Evergreen Plan

- Review accountability agreements for group quarterly.
- Make changes as appropriate within one week of each review meeting.

**Example 13:**
## An Accountability Agreement for an Entrepreneurial Coaching Firm

*(In this example, the Accountability Agreement is used to clarify the relationship between service-provider and client. Within this coaching firm, each of the coaches will also have their own individual accountabilities. Note the results this firm is accountable to deliver, given the required client support.)*

## Business Focus Statement
*(what is the highest-level result we commit to deliver?)*
- Ensure the client is a highly-marketable consultant, workshop leader, and author.

## Accountabilities
*(what broad results are we committed to deliver?)*
- Ensuring that the client works from a clear and holistic business focus, congruent with a deep understanding of personal purpose and values.
- Ensuring that the client develops, and makes decisions from, a strategic three-year business plan, building excellence and integration in purpose, products, and markets.
- Ensuring that the client understands and practices self-marketing in its broadest sense, encompassing all decisions related to product, price, place, and promotion.
- Ensuring that the client is challenged, stretched, takes strategic risks, and is held accountable to the commitments she has made in the development of her business.

## Supports
*(what do we need from the client to achieve our accountabilities?)*
- Complete, honest, and timely communication.
- Willingness to be coached, to stretch, to take strategic risks, and to try new behaviors.
- Honoring financial commitments.
- Willingness to commit the energy and resources necessary to understand the target markets, and to develop products which bring excellent value to those markets.

## Measures
*(how will we know this is working?)*
- Our client's clarity of direction and sense of integration.
- Number of workshops/presentations/other products delivered.

- Feedback from presentations.
- Variety of products tested in the marketplace.
- Number of bookings in target markets.
- Quality of our joint communication.
- Client's willingness and ability to follow through on our suggestions.

## Goals
*(what specific activities will be completed in each 90 day interval?)*
- We will establish goals every 90 days at our coaching sessions.

## Consequences
*(what will follow from our results?)*
*If we achieve our results:*
- The client's business will grow in the direction she desires.
- We will develop a track record in a new marketplace.
- We will both have the opportunity to continue working together.
- We will experience mutual and independent growth and learning.

*If we do not achieve our goals, the inverse of points 1, 2, and 3 is likely to happen, and the learning will be more difficult.*

## Evergreen Plan
*(how will we keep this agreement relevant?)*
- We will keep this agreement alive by spending 10 minutes at each coaching session (and more when needed) ensuring that our work continues to be relevant and on track.

## Example 14:

An Accountability Agreement for the Executive Director of Public Relations in a Community-Supported Organization

## Business Focus Statement

- Secure financial support and drive the image enhancement of the organization.

## Accountabilities

*I am personally accountable for:*

- A public-relations strategy that is widely supported and guides fund-raising and image-enhancing initiatives throughout the organization.
- Developing a three-year business plan for public relations.
- Ensuring the articulation of annual fund-raising priorities and meeting my annual fund-raising targets.
- Programs, events, and communication vehicles that are accurate and reflect a positive image.
- Building pride in our contribution and uniqueness.
- Continually expanding and developing relations with individuals, groups, and organizations capable of contributing to our success.
- Ensuring that the President and others in senior administration are kept informed of emerging and strategic community issues/opportunities.

*As a member of the leadership team, I am also personally accountable for:*

- Ensuring that all initiatives within my department are aligned with the organization's strategic direction, ethics, values, and professional standards.
- The success of my direct reports.
- My own development as a leader.
- A learning environment within my department that is capable of adapting quickly to change.
- Ensuring that I have positive working relationships with key constituents.
- Staying informed of developing trends and approaches.

## Support

- Other directors consult with my department as they build their business plans and network with constituents.
- Invitations to accompany other directors in networking with constituents.
- Early information on any and all matters bearing on constituent relations.
- Funding for the three-year business plan.

## Measures

- Funds raised and business-plan targets achieved.
- Number of constituents I know personally.

- Level of positive and negative media coverage we receive.
- Feedback we receive from potential donors.
- Number and quality of public events.

## Goals

- Complete first draft of business plan by the end of next month.
- Receive final approval for plan by the end of October.
- Conduct one new relationship-development meeting every week.
- Set and meet quarterly short-term funding targets.

## Consequences

- Personal satisfaction from making a significant bottom-line contribution.
- Invitation to consult with and advise other community organizations and institutions.
- Credibility and influence with my professional association, which will bring the opportunity to help develop standards for this profession.
- Developing relationships with interesting and diverse donors.
- Department budget increased to allow for creative approaches and team development.

## Evergreen Plan

- Monthly planning meetings with department staff.
- Annual planning meetings with other directors.

## Example 15:
## An Accountability Agreement for a Young Adult Job-Seeker

*(Following is a unique application of this tool, written by an 18-year-old applying for a summer job. Although it is impossible to write a detailed agreement without prior knowledge of the organization, this template can be used to create a specific Accountability Agreement once a job has been secured. In the meantime, it is an excellent statement of personal promise to the prospective employer.)*

## Business Focus Statement
■ I intend to add value and contribute to the profitability of my employer's company. I am personally committed to bringing a positive, self-responsible attitude to my work. I want to express my passions to the world and make a difference by being of service to others.

## Accountabilities
*I am personally accountable for:*
■ Being on time for work every day.
■ Bringing a positive attitude to work every day.
■ Fulfilling my accountabilities. (I am here to add value, not just put in time.)
■ Being eager to learn and enhance my skills.
■ Working in a cooperative manner with all employees.
■ Serving the customer to the best of my ability.
■ Being a hard-working, reliable, honest employee.
■ Being creative and self-motivated.
■ Working late, when needed, to achieve my accountabilities.

## Supports
■ My employer's trust in me, although I realize I must earn that trust.
■ My employer's willingness to give me feedback as much as possible.
■ My employer's patience, as I have lots to learn and may make mistakes once in a while.

## Measures
■ Feedback from my employer.
■ Feedback from customers.
■ Feedback from co-workers.
■ My personal sense of accomplishment and contribution.

## Goals

- I want to learn more about customers and how to serve them better.
- I am very creative, and want to find a way to develop these skills in my work.
- I want to learn more about bookkeeping and accounting.
- I want to work part time once I return to school in September.

## Consequences

- I take personal satisfaction in knowing that I am doing a job to the best of my ability.
- My raises should be conditional on the value that I add to my employer's business.

## Evergreen Plan

- I would like to meet regularly with my employer and/or my immediate supervisor to discuss my progress in relation to my accountabilities.
- I would like ongoing input on my performance in relation to my employer's expectations.

**Example 16:**
An Accountability Agreement for a Professional Strategic Alliance

*(In this example, two professionals in a long-standing strategic alliance were frustrated by poor communication and lack of clarity about the nature and purpose of their alliance. The "partnership" was close to a break-up, which both would have regretted deeply. Negotiating an Accountability Agreement defined the parameters and limits of the alliance, bringing clarity and renewed commitment to the relationship. In this unique setting, each partner's agreement is the same, since each holds the same role within their alliance.)*

## Business Focus Statement

- We have created and choose to continue our strategic alliance to experience the benefits of:
  - a complementary personal relationship,
  - shared expenses and support services,
  - a unified image which creates marketing opportunities.

## Accountabilities

*As a partner in this alliance, I am personally accountable for:*

- Ensuring that I meet my share of our joint expenses in a timely manner.
- Ensuring that I participate, in a timely fashion and without creating roadblocks, in decisions about our joint infrastructure.
- Building, maintaining, and in no way jeopardizing the image of our alliance in the community.
- Demonstrating respect for my partner's independence.
- Receiving new business opportunities identified by my partner with an open mind.
- Giving and receiving feedback as objectively as possible.
- Ensuring that my partner receives the backup he requests during vacation or other extended absence.

## Supports

- Honest communication from my partner about short- and long-term issues and plans.
- Time commitment to sustain this relationship.
- Respect and understanding from staff on both sides about the nature and importance of this partnership.

## Measures

- Quality of communication with each other.
- Relations between the staff on each team.
- Financial contributions to our joint fund are made on time.
- Absence of tension or stress in the office.
- Regular partnership meetings.

## Goals

- Make a decision with respect to staffing telephone and reception duties by the end of the first quarter.
- Meet for breakfast once a month for the next four months.
- Review our options for lease renewal by next month.

## Consequences

*Positive:*

- We and our staff teams will be happy and contented.
- We will take an annual partnership retreat trip each year.
- Our strengthened relationship will contribute to the financial success of both teams.

*Negative:*

- We experience tension, frustration, and the ultimate breakup of our alliance.
- We experience higher staff turnover.
- We experience less financial success.
- We experience a loss of personal support.

## Evergreen Plan

- We will review this agreement at the beginning of each monthly meeting.
- We will review this agreement (and revise if necessary) every six months at our semi-annual planning day.

# Bibliography

Ackoff, R.L. (1981). *Creating the corporate future: Plan or be planned for.* New York, NY: John Wiley & Sons.

Blanchard, K., & Lorber, R. (1984). *Putting the one minute manager to work.* New York, NY: William Morrow.

Cameron, J. (1992). *The artist's way: A spiritual path to higher creativity.* New York, NY: G.P. Putnam's Sons.

Campbell, S.M. (1995). *From chaos to confidence: Survival strategies for the new workplace.* New York, NY: Simon & Schuster.

Carver, J. (1991). *Boards that make a difference: A new design for leadership in nonprofit and public organizations.* San Francisco, CA: Jossey-Bass.

Chomsky, N. (1996). *Power & prospects: Reflections on human nature and the social order.* Boston, MA: South End Press.

Covey, S.R. (1989). *The 7 habits of highly effective people: Powerful lessons in personal change.* New York, NY: Simon & Schuster.

DesRoches, B. (1995). *Your boss is not your mother: Breaking free from emotional politics to achieve independence and success at work.* New York, NY: Avon.

Drucker, P.F. (1980). *Managing in turbulent times.* New York, NY: Harper & Row.

Edwards, O. (1991). *Upward nobility: How to succeed in business without losing your soul.* New York, NY: Crown .

Fayol, H. (1916). *General and industrial management.* Translated by Constance Storrs. London, UK: Pitman (1949).

Gardner, J.W. (1987). *The moral aspects of leadership: Leadership papers.* Washington, DC: Independent Sector.

Handy, C. (1995). *The age of paradox.* Boston, MA: Harvard Business School Press.

Hendricks, G, & Ludeman, K. (1996). *The corporate mystic: A guidebook for visionaries with their feet on the ground.* New York, NY: Bantam.

Jick, T.D. (1993). *Managing change: Cases and concepts.* Burr Ridge, IL: Irwin.

Jones, J.E. (1972). "Criteria for effective goal-setting: The SPIRO model" in J.W. Pfeiffer and J.E. Jones (Eds.). *The 1972 annual handbook for group facilitators.* San Diego, CA: University Associates.

Kennedy, C. (1996). *Managing with the gurus: Top level guidance on 20 management techniques.* London, UK: Random House.

Kleiner, A. (1996). *The age of heretics.* New York, NY: Doubleday.

Kouzes, J.M. & Posner, B.Z. (1987). *The leadership challenge: How to get extraordinary things done in organizations.* San Francisco, CA: Jossey-Bass.

Kushner, H.S. (1996). *How good do we have to be: A new understanding of guilt and forgiveness.* New York, NY: Little, Brown.

Laborde, G.Z. (1984) *Influencing with integrity: Management skills for communication and negotiation.* Palo Alto, CA: Syntony.

Martin, P.K. (1990). *Discovering the WHAT of management.* Framington, NJ: Renaissance Educational Services.

Peck, M.S. (1997). *The road less traveled and beyond: Spiritual growth in an age of anxiety.* New York, NY: Simon & Schuster.

Perry, T.L., Stott, R.G., & Smallwood, W.N. (1993). *Real time strategy: Improvising team-based planning for a fast changing world*. New York, NY: John Wiley & Sons.

Pinker, S. (1997). *How the mind works*. New York, NY: W.W. Norton.

Reich, R.B. (1991). *The work of nations: Preparing ourselves for 21st century capitalism*. New York, NY: Vintage.

Rogers, C.A. (1980). *A way of being*. Boston, MA: Houghton Mifflin.

Schermerhorn, J.R., Hunt, J.G., & Osborn, R.N. (1988). *Managing organizational behavior* (3rd ed.). New York, NY: John Wiley & Sons.

Scott, C.D., & Jaffe, D.T. (1989). *Managing organizational change: A practical guide for managers*. Menlo Park, CA: Crisp.

Senge, P., Ross, R., Smith, B., Roberts, C., & Kleiner, A. (1994). *The fifth discipline fieldbook: Strategies and tools for building a learning organization*. New York, NY: Currency Doubleday.

Senge, P.M. (1990). *The fifth discipline: The art and practice of the learning organization*. New York, NY: Doubleday.

Vroom, V.H. (1964). *Work and motivation*. New York, NY: John Wiley & Sons.

Weick, K.E. (1969). *The social psychology of organizing*. New York, NY: Random House.

# About the Authors

B RUCE KLATT is a leadership coach, strategist, and systems design consultant with a passion for the practical and a drive to deliver results. Bruce believes that "accountability is the key to building highly productive, vibrant organizations which are healthy places to work and thrive." He is also the author of *The Ultimate Training Workshop Handbook* (McGraw-Hill, 1998).

S HAUN MURPHY is a strategic alliance specialist with a passion for "focusing human complexity." As a cross-cultural consultant, Shaun has worked with business leaders from over thirty countries and extensively in Russia. He is highly-sought as a leadership and team development coach to large-scale projects in North America and abroad.

D AVID IRVINE is a professional speaker and leadership coach to entrepreneurial organizations across North America, focusing on the "human side of business." As Dave says, "We don't have an economic crisis. We don't have a political crisis. We have an accountability crisis." He is also the author of *Simple Living in a Complex World: Balancing Life's Achievements* (RedStone, 1997).

IF you wish to inquire about bulk book purchase orders, if you are interested in contracting with us, or if you want to learn more about our work in organizations, you can contact any of us individually, or you can contact our publisher. We welcome your comments on this book or any other leadership or organizational topic. If you develop a new application for the Accountability Agreement, we would be most interested to hear about your experience.

We can be reached as follows:

Bruce Klatt
Bruce Klatt & Colleagues Inc.
119 Lake Mead Drive S.E.
Calgary, Alberta, Canada  T2J 4B2
phone: (403) 278■3821
fax: (403) 278■1403
email: klattb@cadvision.com

Shaun Murphy
S.D. Murphy Consulting Associates Inc.
Calgary ■ Halifax
Box 21156, 665 – 8 Street S.W.
Calgary, Alberta, Canada  T2P 4H5
phone: (403) 815■4210
fax: (403) 543■6304
email: sdmurphy@agt.net
web site: www.focusing.com

David Irvine

Irvine & Associates Inc.

Box 358

Cochrane, Alberta, Canada  T0L 0W0

phone: (403) 228•0940

fax: (403) 932•7229

email: irvined@cadvision.com


RedStone Publishing

1801 – 8 Street S.W.

Calgary, Alberta, Canada  T2T 2Z2

phone: (403) 228•0880

fax: (403) 245•8725

email: alford@redstone.ab.ca

This is the first book in the **Corporate Toolbox Series**. New publications on coaching and conflict management are forthcoming.

For further information, examples, and updates about Accountability, check our web site at: **www.focusing.com.**

# A Sample Two-Day Workshop on Accountability

## Outcomes:
- Understand the key principles, benefits, and risks of accountability.
- Assess your organization's readiness to work with accountability.
- Plan how to begin building accountability into your work-group or organization.
- Experience working with the Accountability Agreement template.
- Draft your own Accountability Agreement.

## Target Audience:
- Organizational leaders, management teams, human resource and internal consulting professionals.

## Pre-work:
- Participants read this book, and come prepared to write their own Accountability Agreements.
- The group leader (where applicable) develops his or her own Accountability Agreement, to be used and developed as an example during the workshop.

## Agenda:
Day One—AM
*Principles and Mindset*
- The concept.
- The benefits.
- The principles, risks, limitations, and shadow side.
- The leadership challenges.
- Comparison to other approaches.

Day One—PM
*The Accountability Agreement*
- The tool and template.
- The essential components.
- How and where to begin.

Day Two—AM
*Moving Yourself Into Action*
- Write your own Accountability Agreement.
  (with small group and facilitator feedback and revisions)

Day Two—PM
*Moving Your Organization Into Action*
- Assess your organization's readiness.
- Integrate accountability into your work-group or organization.
- Work with sponsors and champions.